Afonso Costa

Afonso Costa
Portugal
Filipe Ribeiro de Meneses

HAUS HISTORIES

First published in Great Britain in 2010 by
Haus Publishing Ltd
70 Cadogan Place
London SW1X 9AH
www.hauspublishing.com

The moral right of the author has been asserted

A CIP catalogue record for this book
is available from the British Library

ISBN 978-1-905791-87-3

Series design by Susan Buchanan
Typeset in Sabon by MacGuru Ltd
Printed in Dubai by Oriental Press

Contents

Acknowledgements

Professor R V Comerford's unflinching support for research has been a hallmark of his leadership of the National University of Ireland Maynooth's Department of History. Not for the first time, but unfortunately for the last, I must thank him for his enlightened attitude. I must say the same of Dr Isabel Fevereiro, who has recently departed from the Arquivo Histórico Diplomático (AHD) in Lisbon. Her knowledge of the archive's precious holdings was unparalleled, as was the help she gave all who used it. She made a unique contribution to Portuguese diplomatic history. My thanks as well to the rest of the AHD's staff, as well as to the staff of the Fundação Mário Soares, especially its Secretary-General, Dr Carlos Barroso. I would also like to thank Jim Keenan, the cartographer of the Department of Geography at NUI Maynooth, who drew the maps detailing Portugal's war effort.

In a busy and difficult year, my wife, Alison, allowed me time and space to write, and held the fort while I travelled to and from Lisbon. For this I am enormously grateful.

My father prepared my research trips to Lisbon, allowing me to make the most of my time there. He and my mother were, as ever, excellent hosts. To them my thanks – and to them I dedicate this book.

Filipe Ribeiro de Meneses,
Maynooth, 2009

Preface

On 26 March 1920, Afonso Costa, former Prime Minister of Portugal and head of his country's delegation to the Paris Peace Conference, wrote to the Portuguese Foreign Minister, congratulating him on the decision to hold an extraordinary session of parliament in order, at long last, to ratify the Treaty of Versailles. Costa, who more than anyone else was responsible for the timing and the scale of Portugal's participation in the conflict, admitted in this document that the Treaty had not lived up to his, and Portugal's, expectations: *I stated openly before its authors that the Treaty is not wonderful – and I did it with such vehemence that on 10 January last, just as it was about to officially come into force, Mr Clemenceau, walking in my direction at the close of the ceremony, and cordially shaking my hands, said, laughing, 'Here is the man whom no-one can restrain', to which I replied, 'Yes, because he is right!' Messrs Lloyd George, Curzon and Nitti, who had been speaking to me, confirmed, with their approving smiles, the justice of my reply.*[1]

Why did Afonso Costa, who had vehemently opposed the terms of the Treaty of Versailles, urge its ratification by the Lisbon parliament? Because he understood that its open-ended nature, especially when it came to the reparations question, allowed Portugal to improve its international standing. This, in turn, would allow him to mount a political comeback, returning to government on his own terms, when he had been forcibly expelled in December 1917. The Peace Conference was, for Costa, the shortest route to the position of primacy in Portuguese politics he had held before and during the First World War.

The Portuguese were, at the start of the 20th century, haunted by the idea of decline. A country over seven centuries old had reached its apogee in the 1500s, when it controlled many of the world's vital sea lanes and strategic points; ever since, it seemed, it had vegetated, watching as the gulf that separated it from the more dynamic countries of Europe and beyond widened. The Portuguese Republic, unveiled in 1910, portrayed itself as the agency that would put a halt to this decline, tapping the energy and talent of the whole population and affirming Portugal's right to live. The majority of republicans, with Afonso Costa at their head, recognized the First World War as a way of hurrying this process. By siding generously with the 'progressive' countries against reaction and militarism, Portugal would earn the thanks of free nations everywhere; its people, meanwhile, would rediscover themselves, the ties that bound them and their potential for greatness. Entering the war would prove difficult, and fighting it was a nightmare. By the end of 1917, few cared about Costa and Portugal's standing among the Allies, and fewer still tried to defend him by force of arms. Ejected from government and exiled in France, Afonso Costa was forced to wait until March 1919 to begin his political comeback. He would fail, however, in this bid for power, while the First Republic self-destructed, paving the way for a dictatorial experience that would last forty-eight years.

The young politician Afonso Costa

I
The Life and the Land

1

A Republic is Born

On 1 February 1908 King *Dom* Carlos of Portugal returned to Lisbon after a long sojourn in his countryside palace at Vila Viçosa, not far from the Spanish border, in his beloved province of Alentejo. With him were his French wife, *Dona* Amélia, and their two sons, Crown Prince Luís Filipe and the younger Manuel. The royal family reached the capital by boat, alighting at the grandiose Praça do Comércio, known in English as Blackhorse Square. There they boarded an open-top carriage for the trip to their residence. To do so, eschewing the safer alternative of an automobile, or even a closed carriage, was understood by the king and his ministers as a necessary risk, a demonstration of confidence by a constitutional monarch in his people. The confidence was misplaced. A still unknown number of armed men stood in the crowd that day. Some, close to the mounted statue of King *Dom* José, fired into the air to attract the attention of the uniformed and plainclothes police on duty. Following this distraction, Manuel dos Reis Buiça, an army-trained marksman, stepped out from the crowd, his Winchester carbine hitherto disguised in a long coat, and placed himself squarely behind the royal landau, at some 10 metres' (11 yards') distance. The king and his family presented an easy target as their carriage moved slowly past the graceful arches of the square, home to the country's ministries, with no armed escort. Buiça's very first shot hit *Dom* Carlos in the back of the neck, breaking his spinal chord and killing him. As the remaining royals struggled for cover, a second gunman, Alfredo Costa, climbed onto the carriage and fired a semi-automatic pistol point blank at the king and his eldest son. *Dom* Luís Filipe was able to return fire, shooting Costa four times. He did so from a standing position, which allowed Buiça, moving now alongside the carriage, to shoot him in the face. He would have shot the queen as well, had he not been stopped by a soldier. In the instants that followed, as the carriage turned left away from the square, *Dom* Manuel was wounded in the arm; the third shooter's identity remains a mystery.

From start to finish, the attack had lasted three minutes. There can be no doubt that it had been the intention of the assassins to wipe out the entire royal family. The result of their actions was catastrophic. Both *Dom* Carlos and his first-born were dead; the queen had escaped, thanks to her frantic attempts to ward off an attacker with a bouquet; and *Dom* Manuel was severely shaken. Alfredo Costa was dragged off to Lisbon's municipal buildings, where he was shot again, this time fatally. Buiça had already been killed on the spot, trying to defend himself from his assailants. *Dom* Manuel II was to rule Portugal for some two and a half years before being swept aside by an armed revolt early in October 1910; on 5 October, the Portuguese Republic announced itself in Lisbon to the world. As a regime, it showed no remorse for the killings, according the assassins heroic status. Who ordered the regicide to go ahead has never been conclusively established.

The 1908 regicide, unique in Portuguese history, did not come as a surprise. The government was engaged in a risky race against time. Its head, João Franco, hoped to create a political movement capable of both dominating the State's apparatus and triumphing in forthcoming legislative elections. Lacking a parliamentary majority, however, Franco had to govern in a dictatorial fashion, relying on royal support for his authority. Often described as an attempt to shore up royal authority at the expense of parliamentary and civil liberties, João Franco's experiment resulted from the desire to restore routine to the political life of the monarchy, then beset by instability as its two dynastic parties, the highly pragmatic Regenerationists and the notionally more left-wing Progressives, fell prey to in-fighting. Their inability to act gave Franco's burgeoning movement its most important selling point: the promise of a revolution from above, addressing the social and economic problems that had long bedevilled Portugal. Franco could only refashion politics and address national ills at the expense of both the dynastic parties and the other important force in Portuguese politics, the Portuguese Republican Party, whose modernising agenda was not wholly different to his own.

All opposing parties had a desire to see the back of João Franco, but no legal means of forcing him out. In a few months there would be elections; given the usual pattern of Portuguese politics, and the energy shown by Franco in pursuing the popular vote, the government would win these elections, possibly with a secure majority. Power and patronage would flow into his fledgling party; he would be untouchable for a time. His weak point was *Dom* Carlos. Were he to be removed, João Franco would be finished. This, then, was the motive for the crime. Its background was the monarch's unpopularity.

Dom Carlos's family, the Braganças, had reigned since 1640, and the king could trace his lineage back to *Dom* Afonso Henriques, who in 1179 was recognized as the first King of Portugal by Pope Alexander III. The monarchy's longevity, however, counted for little. Some of the king's unpopularity was attributable to a lifestyle described by enemies as lavish. In truth, the Civil List, frozen for decades and amounting to less than one-third of its Spanish equivalent, was too limited to meet the needs of the king; most of this money, moreover, was spent not on the royal family itself, but on the upkeep of the royal household and its staff. To preserve some standards at Court, a system of informal advances on the Civil List had been allowed to develop. Rather than dominating politicians through his wealth, like contemporary constitutional monarchs, *Dom* Carlos was largely at their mercy. It was unfairly believed that the king, tall, blond, and blue-eyed, despised his country, and that he preferred to be in the company of his Parisian mistresses. His shyness and the natural reserve of a constitutional monarch were mistaken for contempt. *Dom* Carlos's encouragement of, and participation in, scientific and artistic pursuits were lost amid the accusations of recklessness and immorality that all political factions engaged in since they all, at some point, had been in opposition, trying to overthrow a sitting government. His wife's religiosity and support for the Jesuit order was another source of complaint in a country where anti-clericalism was rife. Her uncommon height did not help matters; around 1.8 metres (6 feet) tall, she towered over contemporaries.

The political deadlock that João Franco was trying to break was occasioned, for the most part, by the paralysis that gripped the two dynastic parties, unable to reflect the needs of a slowly evolving society, to bridge the gulf that increasingly separated Portugal from other European countries and to secure, beyond all shadow of a doubt, Portugal's colonial empire. The country's colonies represented a living link with a glorious past of discovery and conquest in Africa, Asia and South America, against which contemporaries constantly compared themselves. With its peripheral and mostly agricultural economy, Portugal was ill-suited to the challenges of the age. Productivity and incomes were low, and imports of basic items, including foodstuffs, amounted to a constant drain on the nation's wealth. Land was unevenly divided across Portugal. In the conservative north, micro-estates proliferated, affording their holders a bare existence and forcing younger sons into emigration; the restless south was dominated by large estates, where a landless rural proletariat lived in miserable conditions at the whim of landowners. Exports – notably wines and agricultural goods – had traditionally found a market in Great Britain, but were now facing increased foreign competition, and in decline. Attempts to place Portuguese products in mainland Europe faced even greater difficulties, and these were made worse by the protectionist measures designed to protect an incipient, but still inefficient, native industry.

Devoid of iron or coal in exploitable quantities, Portugal was a consumer of the basic staples of the industrial revolution, rather than a producer. All heavy machinery was imported. A recent survey of Portuguese economic development suggests that part of the problem was the inability to find a niche industry suited to Portuguese conditions and resources, that might prove attractive to potential importers; the emphasis was placed instead on competing, through protectionist policies, with industries which already existed abroad.[1] What infrastructural improvements had taken place, notably in terms of communications, were the result of foreign direct investment or loans contracted by the State.

In 1890, as *Dom* Carlos began his reign, Portugal's foreign debt was more than double those of Romania or Greece – although that year's financial crisis would quickly put an end to such heavy borrowing. The saving graces for Portugal were remittances from its emigrants in Brazil (some 650,000 Portuguese left the country during *Dom* Carlos's reign) and some aspects of the colonial economy, with re-exports of colonial goods increasing in importance from 1890 onwards.

The most obvious division in society was literacy: 74 per cent of all Portuguese (higher in the case of women) over the age of seven in 1900 were illiterate. Lisbon and Oporto, where a solid majority could read and write, provided the sole exceptions to this rule; there, however, literacy did not mean support for the ruling order. As the 20th century dawned, Portugal's electoral law, approved in 1899, restricted the franchise to individuals aged 21 or over who could read and write or who met certain property qualifications. The electorate, in a population of some 5.5 million, was restricted by these provisions to some 600,000 people.[2] A narrow elite, whose political rhetoric and basic conceptions were undoubtedly liberal, was loath to abandon the practices that preserved its hold on power, even at the price of making a mockery of political life.

Another feature of the period was the increased tension between the Catholic Church and its detractors. Portugal was Catholic by default, or inertia. The number of vocations leading to ordination was small and out of line with the rest of Europe, as was the ratio of priests to the population. Portugal's colonial empire, capable of absorbing an endless number of missionaries, exacerbated the problem. Nevertheless the State continued to act as a protector of the Catholic

Church, which retained an important role in the registry of births, marriages and deaths; it also controlled a significant business empire and had developed an influential media presence. Moreover, and against the wishes of an anti-clerical minority, the State was increasingly reliant on the Church in order to compensate for its limited coverage of social welfare needs. To increase the number of religious schools, hospitals and old-age homes, legislation banning the presence of religious orders in Portugal was overturned by a Regenerationist government: religious orders dedicated to charity work could now operate in Portugal, but could not actively recruit new members.[3] Many of the clergymen and women in Portugal were foreign, adding fuel to republican accusations of an ultramontane offensive rolling back religious and personal freedoms in the country. In truth, though, the constitutional monarchy had presided over a series of attacks against Catholic interests in Portugal since the 1820s, and the Church was not overly enamoured of this latest monarch, who, while respecting the Church, did little to encourage its activities.

Still less steady in their support for the monarch were the armed forces, which, like those of neighbouring Spain, were burdened by an absurdly high proportion of officers to enlisted men, the latter being drawn essentially from the poorer classes of society, who could not afford to evade their military service. There was no close identification between the monarch and his army, and no overwhelming sense of dynastic loyalty among an officer corps used to the vagaries of barrack life and promotion by seniority. Only African ventures offered soldiers a chance to earn fame and recognition, but their inherent risks made them unpopular enterprises.

There was one area over which a consensus developed in Portuguese politics: the preservation of the country's colonial empire. Nationalist pride and the hope that its colonies might provide Portugal, in the future, with a solution to its financial and economic woes, made it impossible to question the ongoing 'pacification' of the colonies. The resolution of Great Britain and Germany in 1898 to partition those same colonies in case of a Portuguese default on its foreign loans added urgency to the enterprise.[4] The process of pacification would last into the republican period; for a small country of limited means, repeated military campaigns in Angola, Mozambique, and Guinea, and occasional interventions as far afield as Timor or Goa, represented an enormous burden for which the occasional outpourings of patriotism they engendered provided scant compensation. The colonies became a plaything of the armed forces, without which they would have slipped from the country's grasp – and it seemed, for an instant, that such wars might spawn a separate class within the army, contemptuous of parliamentary politics. However, the most celebrated soldier of all, Mouzinho de Albuquerque, for a time tutor to the Crown Prince, was slowly asphyxiated by a political establishment that feared him until, in semi-disgrace, he committed suicide in January 1902.

Not surprisingly, vultures hovered nearby, waiting for the collapse of Portugal's finances before swooping in on the country's colonies. Germany was especially aggressive, but most other colonial powers, large and small, kept a close watch on Portugal's tenuous hold over its overseas possessions. In an unequivocal demonstration of Portuguese resolve, *Dom* Luís Filipe was dispatched in 1907, alongside the Navy Minister, on a tour of the country's African possessions. While most Portuguese were in agreement about the need to preserve the country's existing colonies, there was no such consensus when it came to the ideal size of the empire. *Dom*

Carlos's coronation, on 28 December 1889, preceded by some weeks an event which was to be a watershed in Portuguese affairs: the 'British Ultimatum'. In 1890, Portugal's growing, if unrealistic, hopes for an African empire stretching from the Atlantic to the Indian Ocean clashed with the more ambitious British plans for an unending chain of territories linking Cairo to Cape Town. There could only be one winner, and after a stiff British warning to withdraw from the disputed territories – Portuguese troops were stationed in Nyasaland (today's Malawi) – Lisbon had to back down.

The result was an outpouring of nationalist sentiment, some of which the government, and the Crown, was able to harness, but much of which, being directed against it, spun out of control. The monarchy was described as the Portuguese branch of an international clan, loyal only to its own interests and not to the nation which it claimed to serve. Republicans attempted to capitalize on this sentiment, the very next year launching an unsuccessful uprising in the northern city of Oporto. Calls for a regicide to cleanse the country's honour began to be heard. But equally behind the disturbances was the Progressive Party, which was removed from power as a result of the crisis, and now denounced the Regenerationists, and by extension the king, as subservient to London. When a final settlement with Britain was announced, in September,

One of the more lasting consequences of the British ultimatum was a patriotic song composed by Henrique Lopes de Mendonça and Alfredo Keil, entitled '*A Portuguesa*', which articulated the shame and revulsion experienced at the time and looked forward to a violent reaction against it. This was evident in its final verse, which foretold the day of triumph: 'May the echo of an affront/Be the signal for our resurgence'. '*A Portuguesa*' was adopted by the Republic as the national anthem, although only its tamer first verse is now sung and explicit references to Britain as an enemy have been removed.

protests in Lisbon redoubled. Another government fell, and the offending treaty was repudiated: but its successor, signed the following year, was, if anything, more prejudicial to Portuguese interests. Still, by holding on to Angola and Mozambique, Portugal was left with more land in Africa than it could administer profitably or efficiently.

In 1890, moreover, troubles in the Brazilian economy, alongside a generalized downturn in Europe, spread to Portugal, setting off a financial crisis that would lead to the country's bankruptcy. There was a run on the banks and individuals hoarded the gold sovereigns that formed, for practical purposes, the country's real currency. The opportunity was seized to change over to notes issued by the Bank of Portugal, but Portugal's financial reputation lay in tatters, and the situation continued to worsen. In June 1891, Portugal defaulted on its foreign debts. Only in May 1902 did Hintze Ribeiro's government reach a deal with Portugal's foreign creditors. This suggested the possibility of a large foreign loan, which, given Portugal's political system, was manna from heaven. Whoever was in a position to distribute such funds would be unassailable in power – and it was up to the king to decide who that should be. Not surprisingly, then, those who believed themselves in the running set their sights on *Dom* Carlos. João Franco, a former Regenerationist minister, returned to politics in May 1903 with a new, Liberal-Regenerationist party. It was his aim, he said, to turn public opinion into the true bulwark of political life in Portugal. The party's branches, and their respective newspapers, quickly fanned out from Lisbon. Franco was moving towards a new type of politics, one in which the crowd played a part. Rallies, demonstrations and endless meetings with influential figures and associations filled his days; everywhere he claimed to see a desire for reform and a move away from political intrigue. But Franco knew full well that he could not triumph in elections if he were outside government; intrigue, as ever, was necessary. It was not hard to find allies. José Maria de Alpoim's dissidents from the Progressive Party were one source; the Portuguese Republican Party (PRP) was another.

Portuguese historiography was for a long time fixated on the inevitability of the PRP's rise, accepting at face value the Republicans' own claims to represent an irate and frustrated nation, eager to smash the chains of underdevelopment and ignorance. Such a view necessarily relegated *Dom* Carlos and the constitutional monarchy he headed to the status of historic ante-chamber to the Republic. More recent historians have changed course. By 1890 there were only some forty Republican clubs around the country; only in Lisbon did the party have significant support, among civil servants, officers, sales staff and the owners of small workshops. The very fact that many Republican leaders were in the pay of the State, as officers and civil servants, reveals the extent of the liberal sentiment of the monarchy. The crises of that year showed the Republicans to be divided among themselves, unsure of the way forward and reliant on the Progressives for publicity and funds. The confused uprising in Oporto, which, on 31 January 1891, saw the first proclamation of a Republic, was not directed by the party leadership, and was made possible only by discontent among the army's sergeants, barred by decree from ascending to officer status. The PRP did, however, have a rising star in its ranks: Afonso Costa.

Afonso Augusto da Costa was born in the village of Seia, at the foot of the Serra da Estrela, Portugal's most imposing mountain range, on 6 March 1871. His father, Sebastião, was a local solicitor and a minor player in Regenerationist politics. Costa preferred to remain silent on the matter of his early years. His parents were unmarried at the time of his birth; he was the youngest of three surviving children of this union, which was only formalized through marriage in 1885. Recent research has confirmed a rumour Costa always denied – that he was, in fact, abandoned at birth, only to be reclaimed later by his parents. This unorthodox arrangement might well have been due to the fact that Sebastião Costa had been forced to interrupt his legal studies due to lack of funds – his was a relatively humble family – in order to save enough money to finish his degree at the University of Coimbra. Only once his professional and financial affairs were in order did Sebastião resolve his family's situation.

What all of this meant in practice was that Afonso Costa's childhood was greatly agitated, with frequent changes of guardians and schools. The final year of his studies – he concluded the six years of secondary school in a hurried four – was spent in Oporto, at a religious school. Despite occasional acts of indiscipline, he finished his studies and enrolled in Coimbra in 1887, hoping to follow his father into the law. He was not alone in being catapulted into politics by the British ultimatum, delivered early in his undergraduate career. From anonymity to the maelstrom of national politics was a quick step in such a small country. He collaborated with an older medical student, António José de Almeida, in the first and only issue of a newspaper, *Ultimatum*. While Almeida described *Dom* Carlos as the 'last Bragança', Costa, striking a more moderate pose, wrote about the need to raise the moral standards of the Portuguese. This could only be done, Costa argued, by abolishing the monarchy, setting up a republic, and educating the people: a process he deemed in keeping with scientific progress.[5] Tried for abusing the existing press laws, Costa was defended by Sebastião Magalhães Lima, one of the leading republican ideologues and a future Masonic grandmaster. Almeida was sentenced to three months in jail, but Costa was freed. His academic career progressed, and his prospects within the university improved, despite failing his fourth year as the result of a students' strike which led him not to present himself for examination.

In a curious inversion of his now deceased father's life, Afonso Costa married while still an undergraduate, in September 1892. His wife, Alzira de Barros Abreu, was from a socially more elevated, but equally provincial, background; she gave birth after a year to the couple's first son, Sebastião. Others would quickly follow, and the family became a tightly knit unit. Costa was demonstrating that one could combine academic and professional success with a family life. After he emerged first in his graduating class, Costa stayed at university, preparing his doctoral thesis – quite different from today's dissertations – in the space of five months. 'The Church and the Social Question' was an attack on Leo XIII's encyclicals – notably *De Rerum Novarum* – and was, in essence, a defence of a reformist brand of Marxism, one which preserved a role for the parliamentary process. That Marx was correct there could be no doubt: *Contemptuous of the ethereal theories of utopians, metaphysicians and moralists, Karl Marx charged himself with building his edifice on a scientific foundation. He achieved this, and with such perfection, that neither followers, nor enemies, were able to attack the whole of his deductions!*[6]

Despite the overtly political nature of the work, Costa was awarded a doctorate, and then produced another, more scientific thesis, 'A Commentary on the Portuguese Penal Code', as part of the application for a lecturing post in the faculty. As he did so, he established a legal firm in Coimbra. His lecturing career began in October 1896, with a course on Political Economy;[7] in 1899, at the age of 28, he was given a Chair. In the intervening years, his confidence was shaken by tuberculosis: a cure in Davos, in 1898, was his first experience of the world beyond Portugal. Foreign travel became a passion for him, and he would educate his children abroad, so that they might succeed in life, if necessary, outside Portugal. He continued to lecture regularly until 1902, when, his reputation secure, other tasks finally triumphed over the academy.

By then, Afonso Costa's first political break had come. Having risen quickly in Republican politics – his first intervention at a Republican rally took place in Oporto, on 13 June 1897, protesting against the planned sale of the State's railway[8] – he was asked to stand for the party in Oporto in 1899. An outbreak of plague had paralyzed life in the city that year, the government having imposed a military blockade around it. Oporto's citizens were irate, and, when elections were held in November, they handed the PRP a victory. Three Republican deputies were thus selected; when the election was re-run in February 1900 on a technicality, their vote increased. This particular parliament did not last long, however. This was not a rare occurrence in Portugal at the time. What was rare, however, was the vehemence with which the three Republican deputies – Costa, Paulo Falcão, an Oporto-based lawyer, and Francisco Xavier Esteves, an engineer – attacked the monarchy over what they described as a programme of royal aggrandisement. Costa's parliamentary activity culminated, on 19 June, with a motion suggesting that the constitutional reform under discussion was pointless: what was needed, for Portugal, was a resolute step towards republican institutions. He read his motion, but was eventually shouted down when defending it. As he left the parliament chamber, he turned to the ministers: *To you, gentlemen I will say only this: Rira bien qui rira le dernier.*[9]

Afonso Costa, like most Republicans, did not know how to bring about the end of the monarchy. He hesitated between differing approaches. Contacts were established with the discontented minorities within the dynastic parties – men like Alpoim and Franco – in search of a common leftist front able to challenge the status quo. At other times, however, he seemed to place his trust in armed force. In any case, the PRP had to endure a political drought after its 1900 successes. It would have to wait until August 1906 before it returned to parliament. In the intervening period, four general elections were held, but the PRP had nothing to show for them.

In the meantime, Costa's legal practice thrived. There was no shortage of clients; whatever his political beliefs, Costa's talent as a lawyer made him one of the most coveted legal representatives in the country, and he prospered accordingly.[10] He also involved himself with a number of politically attractive cases, defending those who could not afford counsel. Costa was also involved in journalism, editing, for a time, the Oporto newspaper *O Norte*, and using the pseudonym 'Stry' when writing for *O Mundo*, the capital's leading republican daily. Costa's temper and sense of personal honour, which led to a number of duels and bouts of fisticuffs, increased his popularity, even if one event was to tarnish his long-term reputation – an attack on an older man, Sampaio Bruno, an intellectual with a lifetime's service to the republican cause, exiled after the failed 1891 rising. In 1905 Costa joined the Freemasons, a rite of passage for aspiring politicians in Portugal.[11]

With each passing year, the Republicans' ability to cause

disturbances increased. On 4 May 1906 a riot developed in Lisbon city centre, a republican crowd battling it out with police. Two days later the queen was ostensibly snubbed at the bullfighting ring, when the crowd rose to applaud Afonso Costa, who had arrived deliberately late. It was no longer possible to ignore him, but things did not always go to plan. Costa resigned from the party's ruling body, the Directorate, in 1907, his pride stung by the failure to punish an 'historic' republican, Francisco Homem Cristo, who had insulted him in his newspaper *O Povo de Aveiro*. Homem Cristo would remain a thorn in Costa's side for years to come, especially during the First World War.

The PRP's fortunes were revived by the man whom the party would soon select as its principal enemy. João Franco's first elections, on 19 August 1906, were deemed generally free and fair, and resulted in four PRP candidates being elected for Lisbon: Costa, António José de Almeida, João de Meneses and Alexandre Braga. It was the questions of advances on the Civil List, officially acknowledged by Franco as an established practice, which provided Afonso Costa with a springboard to fame. Out of all proportion, but shocking nonetheless for its audacity, was his claim in parliament that *for a lot less than the crimes perpetrated by* Dom *Carlos I, Louis XVI's head rolled in France*. This bold prediction was delivered at the end of a violent speech, in which he had told Franco that *You, as an administrator, as our executor, have the duty of bringing to this Chamber details of the advances made and to state who benefited from them. The nation orders, and declares it indispensable, that those people repay, without exception, the misappropriated sums, with the respective interest; it also declares that it will not tolerate any increase of the Civil List […] The people also give the solemn warning that the Prime*

Minister must, as soon as everything is paid, tell the King: 'Go, Sire, leave this country, so that, in the name of the Law, you need not see the inside of a prison cell!' [12]

Costa, banned for a time from the Chamber, would hang on tenaciously to the advances question, trying to keep it always in the mind of the public as a demonstration of the king's moral inability to rule. His reputation within the party had been secured. As one admirer put it, in a biographical pamphlet, 'João Franco carried out Justice in the midst of the greatest of injustices [Costa's suspension from parliament] since he took off his mask, in the process displaying the rancorous and consumptive chest of the Monarchy!' [13] There remained, however, no obvious way of ending the monarchy.

As the months passed and his reformist programme advanced slowly, Franco became despondent, and looked for stronger support. Without a majority in either Chamber, and being ultimately dependent on the increasingly uncooperative Progressives, there was only one way forward for Franco to survive: a temporary dictatorship of a kind that had become a common expedient in Portuguese politics. With both dynastic parties having shown their inability to run the country, *Dom* Carlos decided to back Franco. On 10 May 1907, the king dissolved parliament. Franco's new objective was clear to all: to shore up his still fragile party, enabling it to defeat its opponents at the polls and pave the way for the complete restructuring of the political chessboard in Portugal. For the moment, he was still dependent on the monarch; soon the position would change. All parties, from the Regenerationists to the Republicans, began to coordinate their efforts, displaying their opposition to the government and its royal master. Later historians were tempted to see in Franco an early defender of non-liberal politics, a harbinger of Portuguese dictators to come, especially Salazar. But that is not the case: Franco wanted to preside over a reinvigorated liberal regime, in which his party held most of the cards, if nothing else because of the implementation of a new programme in tune with national aspirations.

Republicans, who stood to lose the most from Franco's reformist programme, threw their heart and soul into the struggle against the new 'tyrant'. Franco responded with force. On 18 June, a major clash in the streets of Lisbon left five dead, 100 wounded, and 150 in jail. Press laws were tightened and republican newspapers made to suffer. There were social reforms too, including a law enforcing a weekly day of rest and the creation of a pension scheme for workers. But then, on 30 August, Franco's government decided to forgive the king's debts to the State and increase the Civil List. Such a display of complicity with the king was essential for Franco, whose Liberal-Regenerationists had to plunder the established parties for able members ready to staff the State's apparatus. On the left, however, the move was badly received, and undermined the effect of the government's social legislation. Republicans had a field day with it. Stakes were first raised by *Dom* Carlos's interview with French newspaper *Le Temps*, in which, unusually, he spoke of his support for the Prime Minister and, then, by repressive political measures. Sitting municipal chambers were dissolved and replaced by centrally appointed commissions and the upper house was opened up to a limitless number of royal appointees. The way seemed open to the formation of the new, solid, Francoist party.

Given the far-reaching aims of Franco, and the backing of the king, and given the changing nature of Portuguese republicanism, a conspiracy began to emerge soon after the start of the 'dictatorial' period. This involved Republicans and Alpoim's dissidents, the two factions which had most to lose from the emerging arrangements and which had shown the greatest willingness to disrespect the king. There were even some of Hintze Ribeiro's supporters involved in the planning. Republicans provided the men, monarchists the money; the aim was to subvert enough military units to defeat the police and overthrow the government. Little headway was made. Republicans found it easier to recruit soldiers than officers, and armed civilians – men linked to secret societies such as the Carbonária, whose radical brand of republicanism the staid PRP could not control – than soldiers.

In January 1908 the revolt lurched into action, with contemptible results. Two hundred arrests were carried out, mostly of civilians. Some of the leaders of the PRP were already behind bars, after a tip-off from one of the conspirators. The final assault, on 28 January, was ordered and led by Afonso Costa, but he too ended up in jail. Alpoim made a successful dash for the border. Franco, emboldened by the utter failure of the revolt, decided now to destroy the Republicans. He rushed forward legislation allowing the cabinet to deport to the colonies, without trial, anyone indicted of endangering public order and security. This was a rehashing of his 1896 anti-anarchist law, but was now given a retroactive element: that is, it was introduced specifically to decapitate the republican movement, whose leadership was imprisoned. This was a dangerous step, however, since conditions in those colonies might very well entail the death of the deportees. In the surviving circles of civil revolutionaries, and their more exalted protectors, tempers ran high. Action had to be taken; regicide was the result. The monarchy did not end on the night of 1 February 1908 because no one stepped forward to seize the moment and proclaim a new regime: but it did not have long to run.

After his arrest on the 28 January, Afonso Costa argued that his detention was illegal, as a result of which he would not cooperate with any investigation. He began a prison diary published some years later by *O Mundo*. Piece by piece he turned his harsh cell into a comfortable room, and his meals were delivered by the restaurant Tavares – then, as now, one of the most expensive in the capital: *Today my lunch arrived from Café Tavares. A good fried sole, an excellent veal steak, finely cut potato chips, Collares* [wine], Serra *cheese, an apple, a tangerine and a banana.*[14] From another luxury establishment, the Rendez-vous des Gourmets, came water biscuits. At least, Costa reflected, he could give his weary voice a rest. Five days after the regicide, he was free. There was no conclusive link between Costa and the regicide, apart from the incitement to violence that his spoken and written words undoubtedly constituted.

In the wake of his father's death, all that *Dom* Manuel II could do was appeal to loyal politicians to rally round the throne in a display of patriotism. They paid only lip service to this call; in two and a half years, his reign saw five governments come and go. Franco's political career was finished, and Lisbon had become republican. In the 1908 elections, seven Republicans were elected to parliament; a suddenly conciliatory Afonso Costa was one of them. His party, now dominant in the capital, grew across the country; it had a host of civil associations which advanced its cause, controlled scores of newspapers across the land, had successfully infiltrated the Freemasons and established solid links with, although not control of, the more militant secret societies, such as the Carbonária. Republicans, notably those committed to the violent overthrow of the monarchy, were increasingly confident. The Lisbon populace began dragging the party leadership in its wake and Costa, despite his complete lack of affinity with the capital's working and unemployed poor, decided to follow.

At the PRP's 1909 Congress, held in Setúbal, Afonso Costa spearheaded the drive for a forceful takeover of power. After the Congress, definitive structures were put in place to prepare the move. Attempts began to coordinate action with civil revolutionaries and to recruit military officers – the preference being for an orderly coup rather that a more open-ended assault on power from below. Costa was one of the men charged with this task, but he, like others, met with complete failure, since navy and army officers were not willing to risk their career. Costa continued to press for a coup, nevertheless, with the Carbonária acting alone if need be;[15] this organization's star was on the rise, and it approached the Freemasons for help, establishing in June a 'resistance commission'. Many within the PRP were now worried that they were losing control of events; disconcertingly, Costa now switched over to them. On 29 June 1910, in an interview with the French newspaper *Le Matin*, he returned to his post-regicide line of accepting any government that governed in a truly liberal fashion. With hostility to this stance manifest in both republican and monarchist circles, Costa left the country for the French spa of Cauterets. His larynx was troubling him; a tumour had appeared which he feared might be malignant.

Costa campaigned little in that summer's legislative elections, in which the PRP – against the advice of many now actively preparing a revolution – participated, earning its best ever result: fourteen deputies were elected, including an impressive ten from the capital. Costa returned to Portugal at the end of September. He was summoned to a final meeting of the revolutionaries (some fifty people), on 3 October; it was there that he learned of the plot's details. At a subsequent gathering of politicians, Afonso Costa laid down the basis of the provisional government that would follow the revolution: a widely respected intellectual figure, Teófilo Braga, would be Prime Minister; he himself would be Minister of Justice; José Relvas would become Finance Minister; Bernardino Machado would take over Foreign Affairs, leading the fight for international recognition. António José de Almeida would be Minister of the Interior, charged with keeping order. It is, of course, remarkable that the ministerial dance should be ongoing so late in the day. The meeting ended as the first shot was heard in the small hours of 4 October.

2
Taking Charge, 1910–1914

Afonso Costa did not lift a finger to bring about the triumph of the revolution. He was involved in a confused episode when the horse-drawn cab in which he left the meeting of the night of the 3/4 October 1910 was shot at by some sailors. Six weeks later, this episode would be presented as proof that he *had* been involved in the revolution, and his resolve and determination were praised by *O Mundo* – but it was a ridiculous claim, and one which did a great deal of damage to Costa.[1] While the fighting took place, Afonso Costa stayed in a Lisbon hotel, emerging once victory had been secured.[2] The Republicans' victory was relatively swift and was, in the end, credited to an irascible naval officer, Machado Santos, who decided to make an armed stand, holding a strategic position against government forces and being subsequently fêted as a hero.

The choice of the ineffectual Teófilo Braga as Prime Minister meant that, above all, there would be no cohesion within the government. Each minister followed his own path, in an unashamed race for popularity. Costa was first off the mark when it came to contacting the outside world, signing a communiqué published by *The Times* on 8 October. In it he assured readers that *perfect order and immense enthusiasm* reigned in Portugal and that the machinery of administration and the financial institutions had resumed work. He then outlined the regime's priorities: *We intend to develop education and to make sure our national defences, with the aim of putting ourselves in the position of true and serious allies of your great country. We shall develop our Colonies on a basis of self-government. We shall secure complete independence in the judiciary, and shall establish free and universal suffrage. We shall give all possible stimulus to national economy, and shall establish a real Budgetary equilibrium. We shall make all essential liberties respected, and shall banish all monks and nuns in accordance with our free secular laws. We shall establish methods of social assistance. We shall decree the separation of Church and State.*

Afonso Costa's choice of a portfolio in the provisional government might seem, at first glance, odd, but the Minister of Justice was responsible in Portugal for overseeing religious affairs, and this gave Costa a unique opportunity to reap immediate and rich political dividends. He was sworn in as minister on 6 October, and the following day visited one of Lisbon's jails, ordering the release of all those imprisoned for belonging to secret societies. Afonso Costa quickly imposed an anti-clerical line in the government, to the delight of the civil revolutionaries who had, after all, brought down the monarchy. The Jesuit order was driven from Portugal, and all religious houses were closed down. Costa did not need to draft new legislation; he merely dusted off existing decrees and laws. On 8 October, a mere three days after the regime's proclamation, Costa proclaimed as valid a law dating back to 3 September 1759 by which the Marquis of Pombal, a republican hero, had stripped Portuguese Jesuits of their nationality and forced them into exile. Costa's decree also revived legislation dating back to 1834 which extinguished 'in Portugal, in Algarve, in the adjacent islands and all Portuguese domains all convents, monasteries, colleges, hospices and all other religious houses belonging to all regular orders [...]'.

Costa was not content to legislate from behind his desk: he crisscrossed the capital and its environs, reporters in his wake, interrogating religious figures about their beliefs and practices, and posing as the people's avenging angel, rooting out enemies and showing them to the border. In one famous episode, he left a cabinet meeting, which had ended at 3 a.m., to interrogate the retired Patriarch of Lisbon, Cardinal José de Almeida Neto. Newspaper reports of the meeting make for painful reading, with the bewildered prelate explaining his living arrangements and insisting that 'I always got on well with all governments ...'. When he explained that he would be spending a few days in Spain, but would return, Costa said, grandly, *The Government of the Republic does not drive Portuguese citizens away. On the contrary, it attracts them to the* Pátria *and protects them provided they place themselves under the unambiguous protection of its laws.*[3] On 13 October, Afonso Costa interrogated fifty nuns in one sitting;[4] the following day, 128 clerical detainees held in the fort of Caxias, at the mouth of the Tagus were heard.

Harassing the Church was not a consensual policy. There was, however, no one to bar Costa's way. Monarchists were in disarray and the Church itself, attacked on all sides, could not mount an efficient defence. Moreover, Costa presented his policies as part of an indisputable 'republican minimum', a series of actions which no republican could argue about or question, since they were demanded, or even imposed, by 'the people'. Only shortly before Christmas did the Portuguese episcopate agree on a collective pastoral letter, which was to be read out to the laity, and which, although proclaiming loyalty to the regime, stated that attacks on the Church were also attacks on the nation. Costa, who naturally opposed the publication and circulation of the letter, was able to prevent its being read out in Mass. The one prelate who disrespected this ministerial order, the Bishop of Oporto, was summoned to Lisbon, insulted by the crowd and removed from his diocese by decree. The once hesitant Costa now adopted an intransigent stance, brooking no compromise with those who did not share his brand of republican beliefs – and they were, after all, the majority of Portuguese.[5] In the race for popularity among the republican crowd, Costa also ensured that every legislative step he took was met with large acclaim and celebration. Some of his measures were almost immediate. On 28 October freedom of the press was proclaimed (even if it had largely existed under the monarchy). On 3 November divorce was introduced. A decree dated – for maximum political effect – 25 December 1910 defined marriage as a civil contract between 'two people of different sex who wish legitimately to constitute a family'. February 1911 saw the use of the civil registry made compulsory for all births, marriages and deaths. Costa's popularity was further enhanced by a law improving tenants' rights: rent would now be paid every month rather than every six months.

While these measures were being taken, Afonso Costa surrounded himself at the Ministry of Justice with those he could most trust: José de Abreu, his brother-in-law, headed the Supreme Court's Secretariat; and Germano Martins, a partner in Costa's legal firm, was appointed Director General of the Ministry of Justice. Costa also forged good relations with the War Minister, António Xavier Correia Barreto, who positioned young republican officers in strategic commands and ensured their loyalty and access to the Minister of Justice. Judges who did not toe the line paid the price. The four who failed to indict João Franco, to the great scandal of the republican press, were removed to Goa.

Moderate cabinet colleagues like José Relvas, António José de Almeida and Manuel de Brito Camacho, who had taken over at Fomento (Economic Development), were increasingly appalled by Costa's policies and tactics, which threatened to derail the young Republic. At the same time, a sidelined Machado dos Santos and his 'purists' began to criticize the personalized nature of the regime and, for good measure, trade unions came out in strike after strike. A December 1910 law which recognized the right to strike was not particularly welcomed by the unions since it also authorized lock-outs. In March 1911, a number of striking workers were killed in the southern city of Setúbal by a recently formed national police force, the Guarda Nacional Republicana; they were the first working-class victims of the regime. In January 1911 monarchist newspaper offices were trashed, to applause from *O Mundo*.[6]

It did not escape anyone's notice that when, that same month, a parade was held to applaud the government and protest against recent strikes (in the railway and gas companies), 'volunteer battalions' were on display, a warning to all who might oppose the Republic's progress. Afonso Costa, in command of events, wanted to prolong the provisional government's life, denying that it was in any way dictatorial. Speaking at a banquet organized to celebrate the Tenancy Law, Costa explained his position: *There is a growing trust in the Republic, there are acts of true faith; all of this is explained, sociologically speaking, by the adaptation of the laws to the demands of the collective conscience. That is why our work, far from being dictatorial, is perfectly legitimate* [...].[7]

His opponents in the government wanted to cut short this provisional phase, but seemed powerless to do so. Almeida, in March, published an electoral law that pleased few.[8] Universal male suffrage remained a mirage; so too did single-seat constituencies. As a threat he was, for the moment, neutralised, so much so that, incredibly, Afonso Costa resumed his academic life, securing a Chair in Lisbon's Escola Politécnica. As he could not apply for the position while a minister, he had to take temporary leave from the cabinet, returning to his ministerial position once he had been appointed to the university. Costa's thesis, on the subject of emigration, was immediately published and widely advertized as a work of genius in the republican press. Increasingly contested, Costa went for broke and on 20 April 1911 published his masterpiece of the period: the law of separation of Church and State. By then, a forecast had become indelibly attached to him: *In three generations, Portugal will have completely purged itself of Catholicism.*[9] The day before the law's publication, Costa read it out to an audience composed of Freemasons and members of the Civil Registry society.

Long predicted, the law of separation of Church and State

Afonso Costa's law of separation of Church and State (1911) proclaimed the complete religious freedom of all who lived in Portugal and made it a crime both to coerce people into religious attendance and to disrupt a legal religious ceremony. The Church's property, financial independence and social and cultural roles were curtailed. The number of seminaries was reduced to five. Parish life was organized around lay commissions, from which priests were barred; one-third of the money raised in each parish for religious ends had to be spent on charity. Priests were paid a state pension if they accepted the new dispositions.

became the most important of the hurdles that Afonso Costa would set for 'true republicans' to clear. Those who baulked could be held up to ridicule and contempt; they were, at heart, reactionaries. Costa would later write of the law that it consecrated and defended *efficiently, and against all reactionary attempts, current or future [...] the highest patrimony of the truly progressive peoples – the liberty of conscience and the corresponding freedom of worship.* The law of separation had proved easy to apply because it was inspired by tolerance; it need not be altered in the future *for the simple reason that it is a good Law.*[10] This was blind optimism. By October 1913 only 234 lay commissions had been established, out of 3,800 parishes, and only 20 per cent of the clergy was earning the State pension.[11]

What the French Republic had taken decades and the shock of the Dreyfus Affair to achieve, its Portuguese counterpart had been carried out in a matter of months. *O Mundo* was ecstatic: 'The glorious statesman who studied and drafted this law, Dr Afonso Costa, has just cemented, forever, the glorious edifice of the revolution. This is what can be called building a Republic, organizing a Republic'.[12] Republican army officers scheduled a series of lectures to explain the law to the rest of the troops. Costa went on a tour of the country's northern cities, and was received with wild enthusiasm by local Republicans. The trip to Braga, the country's religious capital, was especially important, allowing Costa to state once more that there could be no understanding with monarchists, or no Republic without the separation, and to do so in the heart of the most conservative province in the country. Thousands awaited him on his return to the capital, carrying him on their shoulders through the station. But these early triumphs would later haunt Afonso Costa. The Church began to fight back. There was a new episcopal protest, and the Pope weighed in with an encyclical, *Jamdudum in Lusitania*, which denounced, condemned and rejected the law of separation.

There was still no significant organised political opposition when elections for a constituent assembly were held in May 1911. Ever since the celebrations that greeted the law of separation, Afonso Costa had been resting, having fallen ill. He did not engage in any campaign actions, but still topped the poll in his Lisbon East constituency. Costa attended the opening session of the Constituent Assembly, in June, the public having been requested to respect his convalescence, not tiring him through excessive contact. His arrival in an overcoat and silk scarf, supported by long-time ally Bernardino Machado, led to prolonged applause. Once recovered, he entered the fray on 27 July, doing his best to shape as radical a Republic as possible and using his illness (but not his leave) as the excuse for the Ministry of Justice's failings and unfinished business. Costa brooked no opposition, and was remarkably vindictive towards those deputies who expressed doubts about his actions so far, but he did not always get his way. The 1911 constitution allowed for the establishment of a Senate which was largely indistinguishable from the Chamber of Deputies (arguments for a corporative assembly – in which representation was carried out on the basis of economic activity, not political party – having been rejected),[13] while the President of the Republic, elected by both houses, was a ceremonial figure, deprived of the power to dissolve Congress.

It was in relation to this office that Costa suffered a defeat whose importance in subsequent years cannot be underestimated. His candidate for the Presidency, Bernardino Machado, was defeated by a more moderate figure, Manuel de Arriaga. This was not a simple preference for one Republican over another: it was a significant warning that the PRP's unity was wearing thin, and that many within it resented Afonso Costa's influence and governing style; within its ranks a bloc was created which took the fight to Costa over the election. Some of its most visible figures, at this early stage, were Egas Moniz, a former supporter of Alpoim, and João de Freitas, with whom Costa clashed violently during the constitutional debates. More heavyweight figures included António José de Almeida and Manuel de Brito Camacho. Throughout July a number of demonstrations and rallies in honour of Costa were organized, their dominant theme being unity in the face of those who would break up the party; this idea was expressed more and more violently in the pro-Costa press, which portrayed the bloc as reactionary and selfish, desiring a president whom it could control. Their campaign was fruitless. All that O Mundo could do in the wake of the elections was to damn Manuel de Arriaga with faint praise and curse those who had elected him, betraying the people and the Republic. The newspaper, more than ever a mouthpiece for Costa, blamed the party's ruling body, the Directorate, for selecting unworthy candidates for the Constituent Assembly, ignoring more meritorious and committed Republicans.[14] In Parliament, Costa and his followers constituted the Democratic Parliamentary Group, establishing a clear division between themselves and the bloc. The defence and implementation of the PRP's vision was its *raison d'être*: as Costa put it, *our aim is to turn the Republic into a progressive form of government, following a policy of maximum decentralization.*[15]

Manuel de Arriaga had made a point of promising that his first cabinet would not contain any members of the provisional government. A sound measure of republican probity, this necessarily affected Afonso Costa's interests, and his Democratic group refused to allow any of its members to enter the cabinet. The Republic's first constitutional government was headed by João Chagas, a renowned republican journalist whose efforts had been initially rewarded with the Paris legation. This cabinet was more moderate than its predecessor, receiving as a result little or no support from Costa.[16] It was also this unfortunate government that had to face the first of many armed challenges from exiled monarchists led by former colonial hero Paiva Couceiro – an ill-conceived and executed invasion from Galicia which had the unfortunate effect of reactivating the civil revolutionaries and unleashing a wave of anti-monarchist actions. There were thousands of arrests and self-imposed exiles as a result. Trade-union militancy also increased at this time, with a general strike by labourers in Alentejo and a sympathy strike in Lisbon.

A moderate government was thus forced into adopting an unpopular repressive line, and Costa used this situation to muscle his way through the October congress of the party, known as the Rua da Palma Congress, where he exacted his revenge on his enemies. Costa argued forcefully for the preservation of the PRP's unity, under a new Directorate, silencing the voices who called for the party to be dissolved. When one member of the Directorate mentioned the splits within the party, Costa interrupted him, blaming the body for those same splits: *It was Your Excellencies who tried to drive us from the party*! Such words electrified the audience, which rose to its feet in agreement.[17] Costa was triumphant, and a new Directorate was duly elected: the party now reflected the views of his Democratic group. In 1912 the PRP split into three. Costa remained the undisputed mentor of the PRP, now largely referred to as the Democratic Party. His more moderate rivals, António José de Almeida and Manuel de Brito Camacho, unable to work together, formed their own parties, usually referred to as the Evolutionists and the Unionists. This unfortunate division would seriously impair the ability of the moderates to oppose Afonso Costa effectively.

Throughout 1912 Costa remained in opposition, secure in the knowledge that he controlled the biggest party in the country and that power would fall into his lap. His rhetoric, if anything, grew more violent and urgent: *Let us not be hypocrites. In the twentieth century the Republic can only be democratic. It was not made to accommodate yesterday's enemies, in all their castes and sects. The Republic was made through the struggle of the people against their masters, against a class which held power and wealth and which cannot thus be called back to collaborate with the Republic [...] This Republic [...] was brought about by the poor and the humble, and it is on their behalf that, above all, it must, act.*[18]

Time and time again the Democrats helped to bring down governments, judging them to be deviating from the path of 'true' republicanism. In November 1912, Afonso Costa addressed supporters in the rural town of Santarém, up-river from Lisbon. While enumerating all that was still to be done (setting out of duties and rights under the terms of the British alliance; balancing the budget; strengthening the armed forces; ensuring that a true republican spirit was present in civil servants as well as in local and colonial officials; initiating the fight against illiteracy), Costa also argued that only a united PRP could deliver on these aims: all republicans must return to the party's fold, leaving normal parliamentary tactics to a later date. The people, argued Costa, had only one thing to tell their politicians: *Return, all of you, to where you were when the Republic was made!*[19] This was easy to say, but by then impossible to achieve. Costa's demagoguery was one obstacle. He described the regicide as a *national execution*, a *synthesis of rage and dignity of a great people*. The day 5 October 1910 had been a *beautiful and unmatchable page in the history of Humanity*.[20]

Manuel de Arriaga's systematic opposition to the Democrats meant that Afonso Costa was only called on to form a government (already the fifth in the Republic's short history) on 19 January 1913. Costa's government, however, needed the support of Brito Camacho's Unionists in the Senate, a weakness which undermined its long-term prospects.[21] He took on the double role of Prime Minister and Minister of Finance. The time had come, he now argued – to the detriment of his radical credentials – to set the Republic on the path of international respectability. The cornerstone of this process had to be balanced finances, which required a disciplined and pedagogical action in the way the State taxed its citizens and spent that income. The party's hotheads were also asked to welcome the mass of monarchist converts who flocked to the PRP, especially in the countryside, forming a network of ex-monarchist *caciques* which would prove vital to future electoral triumphs. This government unveiled a Ministry of Popular Instruction, but had little money with which to build schools and hire teachers. It also established a Faculty of Law in Lisbon (breaking up Coimbra's centuries-old monopoly) in which Costa secured a Chair. By August 1913, Costa claimed, the virtue of a truly republican administration had resulted in a small budget surplus of £117,000. He had already forecast, by then, a much larger surplus for the 1913–14 budget (that fiscal year would indeed close with a surplus of £1,257,000), to be invested in the modernization of the fleet. In a country where budget deficits were the norm, this was a revolutionary departure.

Such steps were not enough. Machado Santos, now obsessed by the return to a republican purity which he believed had once existed, only to be corrupted by the politicians, gathered some loyal men and attempted a coup on 27 April 1913. It was a failure, and resulted in 100 arrests; but it was bad publicity to see the one hero thrown up by the revolution of October 1910 behind bars. Strong action was required as well against the trade unions, which now saw Costa as their main opponent. The ever more common strikes were met with force, the closure of union centres and newspapers and the deportation of syndicalist leaders. A revised electoral law, published in July, restricted the franchise to literate men over the age of 21 not on active military or police service.[22] Afonso Costa remarked, defending this change, that he wanted to build the Republic with informed citizens, not illiterates. This did not go down well. Despite his growing credibility in financial circles, national and international, Costa's popularity was shrinking. A worrying disenchantment with the Republic was shown by the very high abstention rates in the supplementary elections held in November 1913, designed to bring the Chamber of Deputies up to its optimum number. There were, after the elections, 101 Democrats (up 33), 43 Evolutionists (up 2), and 38 Unionists (up 2) in the lower house. There were also 8 independents and Socialists. Brito Camacho, realizing that his collaborative stance was leading to Almeida's greater strength as the voice of moderate republicanism, pulled the plug on his party's support for the government.

Manuel de Arriaga wrote to the three party leaders, asking for their opinion on an independent government which might steer a budget through parliament, revise the law of separation, introduce an amnesty for political detainees and hold the forthcoming general elections. Costa, wary of the manoeuvre, and understanding that whoever organized elections would win them, presented the cabinet's resignation, hoping that popular sentiment would force a solution in his favour. But the reaction to his leaving office was not as strong as he had wished. The Republic was in crisis: no one could govern without the Democrats, but they could not govern on their own either. Piling on the pressure, Arriaga threatened to resign if he did not get his way. Arriaga's solution went ahead, albeit with a head of government whom Costa could trust: Bernardino Machado, recalled from Rio de Janeiro, where he had been sent as Portuguese minister.

3
Portugal at War, 1914–1917

Manuel de Arriaga thought that at long last, with Machado's cabinet, he had secured the much sought after pacification of the republican family. Events outside Portugal, however, conspired to unmask the fragility of this solution. The outbreak of war in Europe in the summer of 1914 re-ignited political passions in Portugal, making control of the country's government more important and desirable than ever. So much was at stake, the rival parties believed, that all means to secure power – and therefore to determine the course of the country's foreign policy, entering the war or remaining neutral – were deemed acceptable.

As happened in so many other countries not involved in the war from the start, a national discussion, sometimes calm, sometimes bordering on the hysterical, evolved around the conflict. Should Portugal intervene or should it remain neutral? Afonso Costa and the Democratic Party believed that it was Portugal's duty to intervene in the war. Military intervention was, in a way, akin to the cutting of a Gordian knot for Costa: an action that would serve to resolve many of the major problems facing Portugal, the Republic, and the

PRP. The war's strengthening of patriotic values would bring the different factions within the Democratic Party, ranging from Lisbon's civil revolutionaries to the staid *caciques* of provincial Portugal, closer together. Military participation alongside the western democracies would improve the low international standing of the Republic; not even the one-off balancing of the budget had led to enthusiasm for the Republic abroad, and Costa hoped that the country's entry into the war would change this. In turn, this would, of course, affect Portugal's internal solidity. A 'republican' war, built on equality of sacrifice by members of all classes, would also help to consolidate the regime in the eyes of the Portuguese people. Finally, the war, and participation in it alongside Britain, France, and Belgium, would remove – it was hoped – once and for all the threat than hung over the country's far-flung colonial possessions, which had, as late as 1913, been the object of discussion between British and German diplomats. It was felt, thus, that one great sacrifice by the country's youth might secure the dream of a safe and prosperous Portugal, resting on a respected and respectable colonial empire. Interventionists saw the increased prestige of the small nations who fought – Belgium and Serbia – and dreamed of foreign headlines of 'gallant little Portugal', fighting for law, civilization, and the rights of small nations. António José de Almeida's Evolutionists also saw matters in this way, although they worried about Portugal's military and economic weakness. Another important interventionist figure was former prime minister João Chagas, who had returned to Paris, and whose official dispatches constituted the most cogent case for Portugal's involvement in the conflict.

Not everyone in Portugal saw matters in the same light. Not even all republicans did so. Brito Camacho's Unionists, from the earliest days of the war, sketched out a different analysis of the best way forward, according to which Portugal should content itself with performing the roles assigned to it by its ancient ally Britain. If Britain, fighting for its life, wanted Portugal to intervene, than Portugal should of course do so; if Britain wanted Portugal to remain neutral, then so be it. Portugal should, in the midst of the chaos of war, stay true to the most basic element of its foreign policy, remaining on good terms with the dominant Atlantic power. To intervene against London's wishes, and without a complete guarantee of support, was nothing short of suicidal. The Unionists would pay for this differing viewpoint, abuse being heaped upon them by the Democrats in the press and even in parliament. The majority of monarchists and trade unionists also stood against a unilateral intervention in the war. The Church urged caution. The small Portuguese Socialist Party was divided.

This tension between interventionists and anti-interventionists was apparent even within Bernardino Machado's own cabinet. The Foreign Minister, Colonel Freire de Andrade, was very close to Brito Camacho's line. For him, intervening in the conflict was unthinkable, since Portugal was singularly unprepared for the challenges of war. His greatest opponent within the cabinet would be General Pereira de Eça, the War Minister, who over the course of 1914 would grow closer and closer to the interventionist position. He did so not out of a political belief in the advantages of intervention, but rather out of pride in the army. The army was in possession of French-built 75 mm guns. These weapons proved their worth in 1914, becoming in many ways the symbol of France's ability to resist the German advance. Knowing that Portugal possessed a number of the weapons, the French army requested their return to France for use against the German invaders. The request was made via London, in order to gain maximum traction in Lisbon; in this manner the delivery of the guns to the French army would be carried out under the auspices of the old alliance.

When the Franco-British request arrived in Portugal, Pereira de Eça immediately opposed the transfer of the guns, arguing that Portuguese weapons could only be present on the field of honour if manned by Portuguese soldiers. He went further, arguing within the cabinet – and these discussions were leaked to the country[1] – that all of the army's branches had to be represented in whatever military expedition was sent to France. The response given to the Allies' request was, therefore, that they could have the guns, but only if they accepted a full Portuguese expeditionary force on the Western Front.[2] The British and the French eventually agreed to this, and in October 1914, at a specially convened sitting of the Congress, Bernadino Machado asked for, and received, the power to take Portugal into the war. Most politicians were aware of the discussions within the cabinet, and understood what was at stake in this decision; it was generally felt that within weeks, if not days, Portugal would become a belligerent.[3]

Incredibly, though, Freire de Andrade was to be proved right. Pereira de Eça, whose obstinacy had caused so much diplomatic activity, had ignored the reality of the army under his command. When mobilisation orders were sent out to assemble a reinforced division to go and fight in France, it was quickly realized that there were not enough men, officers or modern weapons with which to simultaneously defend Portugal, its colonies and a sector of the Western Front. Slowly the interventionist dream dispelled, and the guns, on their

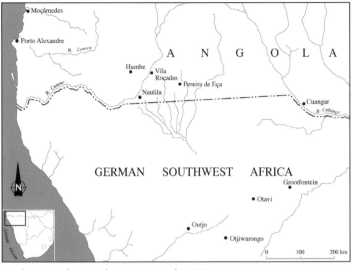

Southern Angola, 1914 (by permission of Jim Keenan)

own, were delivered. It was a fitting end to this sorry saga that the Portuguese guns, although French-made, were slightly different to those used by the French army, firing a different kind of ammunition, and being, as a result, of no use in the war.

The diplomatic situation was made more serious by events on the borders between Portuguese and German colonies, notably in southern Angola. An initial skirmish caused the death of a German district governor and provoked a series of retaliatory attacks on Portuguese forts beginning on 31 October 1914 and culminating in an invasion in November. A recently arrived Portuguese expedition was decisively defeated by a smaller German force which then burned down the fort of Naulila on 18 December. The resulting collapse of Portuguese authority in the border areas was complete, and 1915 would see a major and brutal campaign, led by Pereira de Eça, to re-impose control over the local population, who had thought the Portuguese gone for good.

This sequence of events made one thing clear to Afonso Costa: the Democrats had to be in power. Matters were too serious, and the stakes too high, for an amateurish coalition government to be forever delaying Portugal's entry into the conflict. Only the Democrats, the great organized political force of the Republic, could steer the country to war. As a result, on 2 December 1914, when the Congress reconvened, the Democrats withdrew their support of Machado, bringing about his fall. Surprisingly, and not for the last time, Costa did not claim power for himself. Although a Democratic government was established, the premiership fell to Vítor Hugo Azevedo Coutinho, a second-tier figure within the party. His cabinet, dubbed 'les misérables', was outvoted in the Senate and offered little hope of stability. It soldiered on for a few months until it met with a debilitating challenge from an unexpected source – the army. A large number of officers called on the residence of Manuel de Arriaga and handed in their swords in protest at the political nature of recent promotions and reassignments. Behind this protest lay the fear that a Democratic government would do whatever it took to bring Portugal into the war. With army and government seemingly at loggerheads, Arriaga tried once again to pacify agitated spirits. He appealed to an old acquaintance, General Pimenta de Castro, to form a government designed to hold the ship of state in secure waters until fresh elections could be held. This was a significant step, since the President was refusing to allow the Democrats to organize the long overdue elections.

Pimenta de Castro accepted the challenge, but proved incapable of calming spirits, not least because of his attitude to the burning issue of the day – the war. He made it abundantly clear that he was completely opposed to Portuguese intervention on the European battlefield. The army had to intervene in the colonies, restoring order in Angola, but was to go no further. Since Portugal had not been consulted by Britain over what course to take when the decision to declare war against Germany had been made, Portugal should simply stay out of the conflict and attempt to profit from its neutral status.

Pimenta de Castro went further, granting the widest amnesty seen since 1910, so that even the monarchists who had accompanied Paiva Couceiro in his Galician exile could now be seen in the streets of the capital. This situation was deemed intolerable by Afonso Costa for two basic reasons. First, the PRP was being denied the chance to establish an absolute majority in both houses of the Congress, something it had been preparing for years. Secondly, it was feared that through his actions Pimenta de Castro would make a future understanding with the Allies impossible to achieve. The sooner de Castro was removed from power, the better. In March 1915 the Democrats attempted to reconvene the Congress but were barred from entering the parliament building; they met elsewhere, and called for the overthrow of the government. Costa's words were, on that occasion, unequivocal: *Who could have foretold that, with the Republic in place, there could exist a dictatorship worse, more unworthy and more insulting than that which, within the monarchy, represented that regime's supreme indignity, that of João Franco?*[4]

Pimenta de Castro's government was brushed aside by a violent rising, carried out by armed civilians and the navy's enlisted personnel, on 14 May 1915. This was a considerably bloodier event than the October 1910 revolution and would henceforth be seen as an ideological litmus test by the Democrats: those who had not stood up to be counted on 14 May were not real republicans. Foreign governments were appalled by the violence, sending warships into the River Tagus to protect their citizens and interests; the press abroad was also unsympathetic.[5] João Chagas, who had resigned his position in Paris, was selected as Prime Minister by the coup's organizers. On his way to Lisbon he was shot by João Freitas, whom Afonso Costa had humiliated during the Constituent Assembly debates. Chagas lost the use of one eye and returned to Paris; Freitas was killed on the spot by an angry mob. A favourable government shamelessly manipulated electoral results, and a Democratic-dominated Congress was the result.

Having cleared a path to power, Afonso Costa once again decided not to assume the premiership. He guided Bernardino Machado to the presidency of the Republic, and then stepped back, allowing José de Castro, a republican figure from an older generation, to become Prime Minister. Costa did this for two reasons. The first was an accident suffered while travelling by tram. Hearing a loud bang, he believed himself to be the target of a bomb and jumped out of the moving vehicle only to fracture his skull. Although embarrassing, the incident allowed Costa to distance himself from power, and to show how badly he was needed. The second reason was that Costa was by now completely associated with a policy that he was powerless to implement: intervention in the war. Portugal had failed to answer the Allies' summons in October 1914. The government's task was now to hold the country together while waiting for another British invitation to enter the conflict; bereft of initiative, interventionists were prisoners of the British. It was only at the end of the year that Costa changed his mind, deciding that the time had come to take power. Without any difficulty he elbowed José de Castro aside and created his own cabinet.[6] Presenting this government to parliament, Afonso Costa stressed the need to prepare the country's armed forces and to improve the atmosphere within the army, ridding it of political factions and bettering relations between officers and other ranks. Greater autonomy would be granted to each colony in order to foment its development. At home, measures to increase economic output and reduce the price of basic foodstuffs and other essential items would be taken. In other words, the country was put on a war footing.

Though he met some resistance – Augusto Soares, the Foreign Minister, remarked in that first cabinet meeting that until such a time as the Minister of War assured him that the armed forces were ready for war, there was no point in pressing the issue with London – Costa's timing was perfect.[7]

Submarine warfare was making serious inroads into the Allies' ability to keep their economies going. In addition, Germany had not followed diplomatic protocol, as its minister in Lisbon, Baron Rosen, had yet to call on Bernardino Machado, thus exacerbating tension between the two countries. Then, in December 1915, Britain decided that its weakened merchant marine would henceforth be used exclusively to supply fellow belligerents. It was understood, both in Lisbon and in London, that Portugal, starved of shipping, would have to make use of some of the eighty or so large and modern German merchant vessels which had sought the safety of Portuguese ports at the start of the conflict. Costa's cabinet had many ways of bringing this about. It could, of course, negotiate with Germany for the use of enough vessels to meet the country's needs. This option, however, was never discussed, for Costa saw the new British policy as a golden opportunity to bring Portugal into the conflict. He preferred, in other words, violent action. However, the seizure of the German ships represented an act of war which could not be undertaken without British authorization. What Costa needed, in order to ensure that Portugal was not alone in a separate war against Germany, and that it would be entitled to the full protection of the Allies, was an official British request, made under the terms of the old alliance, for the seizure of the German merchant vessels. This was what the Portuguese government now pointed out to the British, adding the possibility of sharing the seized vessels with London as a substantial sweetener. There were days of tension, even panic, in the Portuguese cabinet as it awaited the British reply. But when it came, and the crisis passed, an ecstatic Afonso Costa ordered the seizure of all the German vessels. This was done in such a way as to cause maximum offence to German sensibilities.

Explaining the measure to the country, Costa said that Portugal had to make use of the German ships for economic reasons, adding that any ships surplus to requirement would be chartered at a commercial rate to the Allies. This was, at best, misleading, since Costa understood full well that most of the ships would be placed at Britain's disposal. Germany responded to the ships' seizure by an insulting ultimatum and, when its deadline expired, on 10 March 1916, declared war on Portugal. Costa's gamble had paid off.

The country at large, however, did not receive the news with joy. A year and a half of war had revealed the character of the conflict: murderous yet indecisive trench warfare on the Western Front was what awaited Portugal, should it decide to participate in the fighting. Nevertheless, for Costa and the other interventionists, Portugal could not content itself with watching from the sidelines; it had to send an army to France, whose governing Union Sacrée Portugal should also reproduce. Costa's vision of who should find a home in this coalition was rather limited. The Sacred Union, for Costa, was reserved exclusively for republicans; it was, at most, a chance for 'bad' republicans – those who had opposed intervention, or had not participated in the 14 May revolt – to repent and to come back into the fold. Negotiations spearheaded by Bernardino Machado for the creation of a new government led only to an alliance between Democrats and Evolutionists, a far cry from what the country wanted. These were, after all, the two most interventionist formations. Socialists and Catholics had signposted their willingness to enter the government, but both were ignored. Monarchists and Unionists were also left out. In a magnanimous gesture, Costa allowed Almeida to take over as Prime Minister, keeping the Finance portfolio for himself. But the ministries crucial for the prosecution of the conflict – Foreign Affairs (Augusto Soares) and War (Norton de Matos) remained in Democratic hands. Norton de Matos, in place since May, now accelerated the on-going preparation of a Portuguese expeditionary force destined, it was hoped, for the Western Front.

Afonso Costa's logic for entering the conflict was close to what in the Italian case would be described as 'democratic interventionism': using the conflict to strengthen the republican tradition in Portugal and to defeat once and for all what he identified as the remnants of reaction within the country. There was never, on his part, any acknowledgement of the fact that this was a high risk strategy, and there was little discussion about the country's ability to withstand the shock of war. The Sacred Union government shared the view that Portugal should participate as fully as possible in the conduct of the war – on sea, in Africa and on the Western Front. To this end, Norton de Matos had long been preparing a division to be sent to France; he now sought to dispatch another expedition to East Africa, where General von Lettow-Vorbeck and his *Askaris* were still defying the Allies. The resources of the Portuguese army were stretched as a result of the desire to fight two different wars in very different conditions. Since no Allied request for the use of Portuguese troops in France seemed forthcoming, the Portuguese concentrated first on

José Mendes Ribeiro Norton de Matos (1867–1955) was a latecomer to republican politics. He nevertheless served as Governor-General in Angola from 1912 to 1915, returning there as High Commissioner in the early 1920s. He would be a prominent figure in the opposition to Salazar, running for the presidency of the republic against Salazar's incumbent, General Carmona, in 1949. As Minister of War from 1915 to 1917, Norton de Matos organized the Portuguese Expeditionary Corps and oversaw its dispatch to France, but was unable to rid it of political infighting or to imbue it with a true *esprit de corps*.

Mozambique, sending the largest ever expedition to the colony to mount an invasion of German territory. This did not mean the end of the dream of sending troops to France, which remained the priority, to be pursued diplomatically. What eventually made this dream possible was not a sudden change in the Allied estimate of Portugal's military capability, but rather the fact that over the course of 1916 the war became, more than ever before, a simple matter of attrition, and that men were sought wherever they could be found.

António José de Almeida's government was not seen by the Allies as particularly effective or efficient. The two parties and their respective newspapers did not warm to each other, and cabinet insecurity was a constant. France's minister to Portugal, Emile Daeschner, fumed at the delays encountered by the government in Lisbon as it sought to prepare the country for war. The use to be made of the German ships was one problem; the fate of enemy aliens and their property was another. It was only thanks to the efforts of Costa and Almeida that the Sacred Union continued to exist. Cooperation and goodwill between the two former rivals now developed, and this would remain in place for years to come, although it was misunderstood, and in some cases resented, by their respective parties. Their cooperation failed, however, to resolve the pressing issues that entry into the war had caused. Portugal, reliant on the outside world for food and energy, was not faring well as the war's economic grip tightened. Inflation and shortages of essential goods, notably wheat and coal, brought on social turmoil. That the border with Spain leaked like a sieve made matters worse, since food smuggling became common (it also made evading military service easier). Prices on the black market were naturally higher than those set by the government. What all this revealed was the weakness of the State and its inability to enforce crucial decisions; reliance on the patriotism and abnegation of the population was misplaced. On 9 October 1916 the director of postal censorship reported on the country's mood, as evidenced in intercepted letters, concluding that:

1. The war is not popular;
2. There is a marked spirit of revolt against the idea of our fighting in foreign territory;
3. There are those who believe that it is probable that a revolutionary movement will prevent the departure [of the troops] for war, or will follow on from it;
4. In Africa, in Kionga, a serious military disaster has taken place;
5. The sanitary conditions of the troops in the colonies are precarious;
6. There has been hunger in the colonies, even among the soldiers.[8]

As 1916 came to an end the situation worsened. After capturing the disputed territory of Kionga, Portuguese forces under General Ferreira Gil crossed into German East Africa in September and moved towards the inland town of Newala, which they captured late in October. It was only then that they realised that they had fallen into a trap, being surrounded with no access to water. Within a few days they had fled the town and made for the border, with the Germans in pursuit. Ravaged by disease, the Portuguese were at the mercy of their enemies. Word of the disaster at Newala began to filter back in December. Opposition newspapers blamed the government and its leader for the attempt to run the campaign from Lisbon, and for the political appointment of an

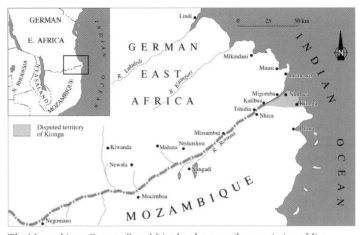

The Mozambique-German East Africa border, 1914 (by permission of Jim Keenan)

inexperienced commanding officer. Just as serious, in political terms, was a major coup attempt, organised by the 'hero' of 1910, Machado Santos. By now an inveterate conspirator, Machado Santos was able to put together a plot which linked discontented military figures, monarchists and trade unionists. The movement was a complete failure, but although publicly the government gloated over the ease with which Machado Santos was defeated, in private ministers recognised that events might well have taken a different turn.[9] As the year drew to a close, legislation was passed which allowed the cabinet to dismiss officers and non-commissioned officers charged with crimes of 'treason, espionage, insubordination, revolt, military sedition and cowardice', and to hold them without trial for as long as the war lasted. This controversial law was drafted in such a way that its provisions covered the recent rising, which meant, in effect, that the principle of retroactivity was ignored. Some Evolutionist deputies found this too much to take, aligning themselves with the Unionists and reviving the old bloc.

The year 1917 thus began against a troubled political background. There was, however, some good news for António José de Almeida's government: a force was finally dispatched to Flanders. On 17 January a decree transformed the existing Instruction Division, which had undergone a period of intense training, into the Portuguese Expeditionary Corps (CEP), and appointed as its commanding officer General Tamagnini de Abreu, a politically reliable senior officer who had commanded the regime's new police force, the Republican National Guard (GNR). The delay in the troops' departure had been caused by the low priority assigned to their transport by the British Admiralty. What London did not understand was that the delays fuelled rumours that the army would never actually leave Portuguese shores, making the government's task much harder. Tension between Lisbon and London on this issue would remain a constant throughout 1917: the Portuguese accused the British of ill-will while the British stressed the poor organisation of the Portuguese, which had led to the precious vessels carrying fewer soldiers than they should have done. In early February the first Portuguese troops arrived in France to receive further training. It was only on 10 July that the 1st Division took over the three brigade sectors allotted to it. To ensure the Portuguese forces a greater degree of independence, and a constant presence at the Front, the CEP's command requested the dispatch of a second division, turning the Portuguese force into a full army corps. The government quickly agreed.

While Portuguese troops in France prepared for combat, the political situation in Portugal worsened. In April, one of António José de Almeida's pet projects – a forum bringing together the government and the country's economic elites – led to the fall of the cabinet at a time when Almeida was ill and Afonso Costa was abroad at an Allied economic summit. A poorly attended parliamentary session saw the Evolutionist Minister of the Economy, Fernandes Costa, turn the matter into a vote of confidence in the government, only to see it defeated by 57 votes to a paltry 21. Did Afonso Costa play any role in the fall of this government? He always argued the contrary, describing the event as the first blow by his opponents within the party, men whose ambition was fuelled by the government's collective loss of popularity. Alexandre Braga, who would serve as Costa's domestic mouthpiece in the years following the First World War, would remark, at the PRP's Congress of December 1920, 'The first political act in the destruction of the so-called "Sacred Union" was carried out one or two days before the well-publicised return of Dr Afonso Costa from abroad, and all my efforts as party leader in the Chamber to convince its promoters to delay their action for 24 hours, so that Dr Afonso Costa might have been made aware of such a grave resolution, and be heard on the subject, were insufficient.' [10]

Not all Portuguese and diplomatic observers agreed in April 1917 that this was the case. Opposition figures claimed that Afonso Costa had pulled strings in the affair; Costa's old bugbear, Homem Cristo, wrote that Almeida had been treated as 'ballast, a contemptible being, a poor devil'.[11] The practical result of the crisis was a severe weakening of the Sacred Union. A new government was formed under Afonso Costa's leadership, consisting solely of Democratic ministers. António José de Almeida promised his party's support, but all the responsibility for the war would henceforth rest on a single set of shoulders: Afonso Costa would stand or fall in accordance with Portugal's war effort.

Minutes of the Council of Ministers reveal that there was not one moment's peace for this troubled government. Costa and his colleagues (notably Norton de Matos and Augusto Soares, who retained their ministerial portfolios) were under the most intense pressure of their careers. Supplies were the most pressing issue, since the availability of bread in the cities, especially Lisbon, was precarious. At times reserves fell to only three days' worth, and these could only be topped up by requisitions in the countryside, which were enforced at a high political cost – too high for many municipal administrators, who resigned rather than enforce government policy. Expensive foreign wheat was also resorted to in an effort to stave off starvation; colonial maize, while available, was difficult to transport, and there was almost no coal with which to fuel the ships for the colonies. The lack of food, coal and shipping, together, implied the shelving of all possible initiatives for the development of the country; only a swift Allied victory could overturn this dismal scenario. The worsening food situation also had implications for public order, with major food riots in Lisbon in May. General Pereira de Eça, who had 'pacified' southern Angola in 1915, was now military governor of the capital: when the government suspended constitutional guarantees in the city and its environs, his troops moved in to restore order. O *Século* reported the deaths of 23 men and women and the wounding of another 50; British estimates of casualties were much higher.[12] There were other worrying developments. The situation in Africa grew bleaker with each passing day. Álvaro de Castro, Governor-General of Mozambique, sent regular appeals for money and more troops: there were local insurrections to deal with and von Lettow-Vorbeck led his army into Portuguese territory late in November 1917.

Afonso Costa disappeared from sight during these months. Gone were the days of his whirlwind fact-finding trips across the country, and of a popular following. Portugal's Prime Minister worked long hours to try to resolve the country's myriad difficulties, and used his family and close associates as a filter, keeping complaints at a distance. His participation in wartime propaganda was practically non-existent. This distance from the public and its concerns might well be to blame for the decision to increase the size of the CEP. In July, having convinced the British military authorities to accept his scheme, Norton de Matos announced that the CEP would become an independent army corps of 55,000 men. Incredibly, he went on to explain that such a force would require a monthly reinforcement of some 4,000 men in order to maintain its strength. The statement provoked an outburst of anti-government sentiment, since it described an open-ended, and entirely voluntary, bloodletting on Portugal's part, without any agreed recompense. The time had come, the bloc said, to review the conditions under which Portugal had gone to war. The time had come, in other words, for secret sessions of the Congress in which the discussion could be open, frank, and far-ranging.

The secret sessions of both houses of parliament took place from 11 to 26 July 1917, coinciding with a construction workers' strike that turned violent and once again led to a suspension of constitutional guarantees and widespread brutality by the security forces. The sessions were not Afonso Costa's finest hour, since he had much to cover up – including mistakes that were not of his doing – in order to preserve good relations with the army. Moreover, he was forced to rely on his majority to prevent parliamentary inquiries being carried out into the reasons for Portugal's belligerence and the conduct of the war. While this made practical sense, the political damage was great, since the bloc couched its attacks as a defence of parliament's prestige. Afonso Costa had also to rely on personal insult against Brito Camacho, whom he accused of seeing the war as a mere business transaction and not, as it really was, a matter of life and death: *Brito Camacho has been unhappy. It is his fate. He can only carry out bad deeds. Always bad deeds. I cannot ask him to reconsider. Keep going: one day remorse will come* [...][13]

The government reached its nadir when a Democratic deputy read out a series of sworn statements regarding the behaviour of the Pereira de Eça column in Angola, back in 1915. These statements described terrible atrocities which undercut any sense of a Portuguese civilising mission in the area: Portuguese rule there now rested solely on terror. The opposition naturally requested an inquiry, but the government blocked this: the charges were too serious to be aired publicly. What this meant, however, was that Afonso Costa was now protecting the army – which had little love for him – from parliament, his natural base of support. Moreover, he was doing so at a time when the population of Lisbon were deprived of their constitutional rights and subject to the will of their military governor, General Pereira de Eça, the same officer whose troops had been accused, in convincing terms, of conducting a savage and inhuman campaign. Costa's words were hardly inspiring: *We must not be moved by idealism or forget the concept, or the estimate, that blacks have of humanitarian respect, which they view as weakness or pusillanimity.*[14]

Costa's stance led the opposition to walk out of the secret sessions before one last burning issue was discussed: the use made of the seized German ships, most of which (and not some, as initially suggested by Costa) had been chartered by a British shipping company, Furness Withy, in a deal which many in Portugal thought ruinous. After the secret sessions, any hope of working with the opposition was shelved. Brito Camacho bypassed the Chamber of Deputies and went straight to the press: 'Look at what happened in Africa […] We suffered a disaster in Naulila, we suffered a disaster on the Rovuma, and we suffered a disaster in Newala, and on none of these subjects has the country been given any explanations by the government.'[15] His conclusion was dramatic: change was imminent, and if it did not come via legal means, it would come through revolutionary action.

Brito Camacho was fully aware that such action was being planned by members of his party. When it came, it did not need much force. Costa had lost the support of the man in the street. In August a Lisbon water-workers strike left the capital parched during the hottest month of the year. Later that month the government mobilised striking postal workers, many of them former 'civil revolutionaries' for whom a position had been found as a reward for services to the Republic, so that industrial action was equated with desertion. Those among them who had been spared military duty on account of their key positions were now ordered to join their units. The national trade union movement, the União Operária Nacional (UON), declared a general strike in protest, and was backed by all segments of the opposition. Although keeping the mobilization order in place, the government eventually backed down: salary rises were agreed, and not a single postal worker was sent to the Front.

When one considers this episode, and the lack – and inadequacy – of war propaganda in Portugal, one is left with the impression that Afonso Costa was completely unaware of what it took to keep a country at war, and miscalculated the degree of sacrifice he could ask the country to make. The decision to increase the CEP's size seriously strained the country's military resources, besides adding to the transport difficulties involved in keeping the expeditionary force properly supplied and reinforced. The British were singularly unimpressed by their Portuguese allies, who at one point, with their two divisions stationed side by side, held 16 kilometres (9.9 miles) of the Front Line. Lord Derby, Minister of War, proposed that a single division remain at the Front, as part of a British army corps, while the other rested behind the lines. More woundingly still, Derby suggested that, as had been the case during the Napoleonic Wars, British officers might be allowed to serve in the Portuguese army. Norton de Matos was furious,

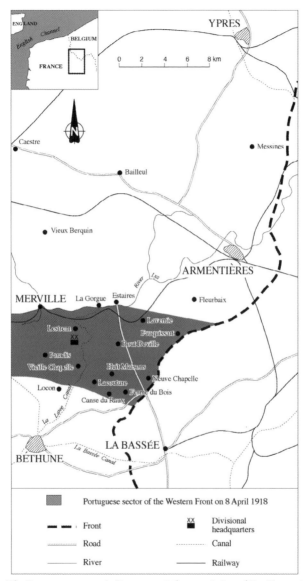

The Portuguese sector in France, 1918 (by permission of Jim Keenan)

and his reply showed it;[16] but he knew full well that the CEP was becoming unmanageable.

On 17 May 1917, at a time when Norton de Matos was in London, Afonso Costa cabled him, stating that, *If you do not obtain an absolute victory on the subjects of the army corps and of the troops' transport aboard British ships, and if difficulties with securing a loan continue, to the detriment of our national existence, as was tragically demonstrated a few days ago, the Portuguese government will be forced to explain the situation to the country and immediately resign in recognition of the error made by some of its members.*[17] Some weeks later it was Norton de Matos who cabled: 'The situation caused by the lack of officers is deplorable and very grave; we cannot go into combat and the English [*sic*] Ministry of War questions our wish to constitute an army corps and our hurry to ship more troops if we do not even have enough officers for those troops already in France.'[18]

The 2nd Division was never as well constituted as the 1st. The British, losing patience, slowly withdrew their fast transport ships from Portuguese service until, at the end of October, there were none. With the war still raging in Mozambique, increased rates of desertion from the army in Portugal, the coming of winter in Flanders and the lack of suitable ships to reinforce the CEP, Tamagnini de Abreu's task was fast becoming impossible. In January 1918 he warned Lisbon that he needed 9,000 men to plug the holes in his line and to create a reserve force of 4,000 men, promised to the British but never actually constituted.[19] A visit to the Front Lines by Bernardino Machado and Afonso Costa in the autumn, after a visit to London and Paris, brought no comfort to the hard-pressed troops.[20]

Domestically, moreover, there was no good news to be had.

Within the Democratic Party there was agitation, and many looked to the deputies who had gone to the Front to clean up the party and form a new government. Local elections and a few by-elections were remarkable for their enormous abstention rates, and a resurgence of conservative forces; Marian apparitions at Fátima, which electrified Portuguese Catholics, confirmed that a religious fight-back was now underway; and throughout the country anti-government and anti-war propaganda was rife. A pamphlet entitled *Rol da Desonra* (Dishonour Roll), supposedly written by officers serving on the Western Front, was widely distributed by monarchist conspirators. This infamous publication detailed the nature of life in the trenches, contrasting it with the easy life led by those members of the CEP who, through their political connections, allegedly stayed at the rear and in Paris. Sebastião Costa, Afonso's eldest son, was one such figure.

By late November the Minister of the Interior was warned that in the district of Viseu: 'there is absolutely no respect either for the authorities or the public servants. The working classes, as the result of a miserable sort of propaganda, carried out openly by the institutions' enemies [...] blame the authorities and the public servants for this high price of foodstuffs. Everyday large groups form and provoke all who pass before them, continuously causing disorder.'[21]

Finally, the food situation was once again calamitous. On 28 October *O Século* cautioned that 'we are living off the scarce remains of the national harvest, which will last for a few weeks more. After that there will be hunger [...]'. The Lisbon daily added that even these last remains of grain had to be pried from the hands of farmers. This was not scaremongering: in November, Bernardino Machado informed the French minister that Lisbon was facing an imminent and complete collapse in the supply of bread; the French diplomat cast doubt on the good that emergency foreign supplies might achieve, given the inefficiency and corruption of the machinery in place to distribute food: '[…] in my opinion it must be remembered that a Portuguese government would hardly have the authority or the necessary means to enforce any sort of food regulations, and the situation is serious.' [22]

The final months of 1917 were the most difficult of the First World War for the Allies. The Bolshevik victory in Russia spelled the end of the Eastern Front; a Franco-British intervention was needed to stabilize the Italian line after the disaster at Caporetto; and in France, the Sacred Union, exhausted, reached its end, making way for a government led by the veteran Georges Clemenceau. In such circumstances, the drama about to enfold Portugal was to pass largely unnoticed; but for the men who fell from power, Afonso Costa at their head, the events of December 1917 spelt the ruin of the effort to strengthen the young republican regime through a dedication to the essential values of the Allied cause. For Afonso Costa, what came to be known alternatively as *dezembrismo*, *sidonismo* or the 'New Republic' was a calamity and an act of inexplicable and unforgivable treason. It would be impossible for him, as a politician, to overcome the impact of those months. Henceforth, his political action would be dedicated to the return of Portugal to the lofty position Costa believed the country had reached in the very first days of December 1917, thanks to his guidance.

On 18 November, Afonso Costa and Augusto Soares, with their respective spouses and staff, left for Paris in order to attend an Inter-Allied Conference devoted to economic and financial issues designed to resolve the economic and financial difficulties being experienced by the war-weary Allies.

Expectations were high among the Portuguese delegation, but Afonso Costa was forced to spend more time in Paris, where he arrived on 21 November, than he had wanted to, and indeed than conditions in Portugal allowed for. The political crisis in France and David Lloyd George's busy agenda led to the postponement of the conference's opening, which occurred only on 29 November. In the intervening days the Portuguese premier made a number of visits, including to some Portuguese units. Apart from Costa, Lloyd George and Clemenceau, five other heads of government were present, representing Belgium, Greece, Italy, Montenegro and Serbia. The United States was represented by Woodrow Wilson's foreign policy advisor, Colonel House. After a short welcome, Clemenceau handed over to his Foreign Minister, Stéphen Pichon, who proposed the creation of five separate commissions: Finance, Armament and Munitions, Imports and Maritime Transport, Supplies, and Blockade.

On 6 December, some days after the Conference's end, *Le Temps* published the resolutions approved by the different commissions. The Finance commission, for example, had resolved to hold periodic meetings in order to monitor and solve problems related to credit, exchange, and inter-Allied payments. The Imports and Maritime Transport and the Supplies commissions had issued a common resolution: an inter-Allied organization would be established to rationalize available resources – ships and supplies – in order to meet the needs of the various countries while freeing up as much shipping as possible to transport the American army to France (America had declared war on Germany on 6 April 1917). Portugal had played a substantial role in this, thanks to the German ships seized in 1916.

The importance of the issues under discussion kept Costa

in Paris. His negotiating performance is one of the central planks of his reputation. On 30 May 1921 José de Abreu published, in O *Mundo*, an account of the Paris conference and what happened next. Of Costa's achievements, he wrote, 'Dr Afonso Costa strove to obtain, and succeeded in doing so, among other things, the restitution by Britain of up to 100,000 tons of the shipping we had seized from Germany, and the opening of credit lines by Allied exporting countries, including Britain and America, for the supply to Portugal, *for the whole of the war and until one year after the signing of the armistice, without immediate cost and to be reimbursed only after the end of the war*, of the coal necessary to the life of the country, the quantity having been fixed at one and a half million tons/year, and of the wheat needed to make up our cereal shortfall, the quantity having been fixed at 240,000 tons/year.' This was not all: Portugal had been designated a priority country for German reparations payments, both in terms of scheduling and of the sums to be paid.

If all of these claims are true, then this would have been an historic event for Portugal and the highest point of Costa's career. Most of the troubles endured by Portugal since the start of the war would have been overcome: enough food for every family, coal to power the economy and ships to supply both the country and its armed forces and to allow Portuguese exporters to reach their markets. However, there is no confirmation that such specific guarantees were indeed given to Afonso Costa by his Allied counterparts in the relevant file in Lisbon's Arquivo Histórico Diplomático or in the Portuguese *White Book* (a collection of documents on Portugal's intervention in the First World War published, in incomplete fashion, in 1920). And although Costa would henceforth refer to the 1917 conference as the pinnacle of Portugal's international standing, he did not bring up the concessions at the Versailles Peace Conference, while some of the claims advanced by Abreu make more sense in 1921, when they were published, than they did in 1917. Lastly, if the concessions were made to Portugal, rather than to Costa personally, then they should have been renewed to his successors, which was not the case.

Once the conference was over, Costa belatedly headed home. On 5 December he was at Hendaye, on the Franco-Spanish border, where a hospital for Portuguese troops had been installed with funds raised by the Portuguese Women's Crusade. That afternoon he and his party set off for Lisbon, unaware of what was, by then, occurring in the Portuguese capital. The night was spent crossing Spain, and Portugal was reached in the early hours of 6 December. It was later in the day, in the small station of Fornos, that word of an armed revolt in Lisbon finally reached the Prime Minister; Afonso Costa was asked to wait at the station until the Civil Governor of Guarda arrived with more concrete information. Costa then pushed on to Pampilhosa, near Coimbra, where the local Civil Governor was waiting for him with instructions from Norton de Matos not to let Afonso Costa return to Lisbon, arresting him, if necessary, should he insist on continuing the journey. Visibly impressed, Costa diverted to Coimbra. From there he established telephone contact with the embattled Norton de Matos, who told him that a revolt had broken out but that he expected to restore control of the capital the following day. Costa also spoke with his daughter Maria Emília, advising her to leave the family home and find a safe refuge.

The following morning, on contacting Norton de Matos, Costa was told that the final assault against the rebels was about to be launched, and that he should head for Oporto in order to ensure that the city remained loyal. Arriving there in the evening, Costa's party was informed that the government was victorious in Lisbon, and so dined in peace, celebrating what they thought was victory – only to be told by the arriving Civil Governor of Oporto, at the end of the meal, that this was not the case: the government had, in fact, resigned. Rushing to the Civil Governor's office, Costa telephoned Bernardino Machado, whom he castigated for accepting the cabinet's resignation without first contacting him. Why had he done so? According to José de Abreu, because Norton had told Machado that if he did not accept the collective resignation, then every single minister would, one by one, resign in person.[23] The incident left a sour taste in Costa's mouth, since naturally he believed he should have been consulted over the fate of his own government.

He returned to his hotel, where he spent a difficult night. Thoughts of resistance were soon dispelled and apprehension about his safety began to grow. Friends offered their houses as a hiding place. On 8 December he signed a letter sent by his wife to their children, informing them that they were both well and asking for news. That evening, he was arrested as part of a city-wide sweep ordered by the coup's leader, Sidónio Pais.[24] Within a few days, as friends worried about his wellbeing, he was sent – by sea – to the prison at Trafaria, opposite Lisbon, where he was held for four days. The *Diário de Notícias* informed its readers, on Costa's arrival, that it seemed as if he would soon be sent to a remote location. On 17 December he boarded a steamer, escorted by a detachment of Infantry 33, a regiment which had joined the coup instead of setting off for France. According to a journalist, 'his wife and daughter, who had been to visit him today, watched his embarkation and were visibly impressed by the departure of their husband and father.' [25] Once aboard, Costa shouted *Long live Portugal! Long live the Republic! Long live Portugal's participation in the war!* He reached Elvas, on the border with Spain, aboard a special train: a first-class compartment, which he had to himself, and a third-class compartment, where his armed escort – again, drawn from Infantry 33 – travelled. There he was held incommunicado. Afonso Costa's war was over.

President Machado and Prime Minister Afonso Costa of Portugal in October
1917

II

The Paris Peace Conference

4

Waiting in the Wings, 1918–1919

Afonso Costa's detention in Elvas was a traumatic experience for the closely knit Costa family. Their home in Lisbon was twice sacked by a mob, and its contents were stolen or destroyed. His brother Artur was also in jail as a preventive measure; over Afonso's wife there hovered an accusation of misappropriation of public funds destined for the Portuguese hospital at Hendaye; everywhere insults against Afonso Costa could be heard and read, and there were fears for his life. On 23 January 1918 the *Diário de Notícias* published a letter written by Alzira Costa. In it she denied a story carried by two Oporto newspapers to the effect that her husband had tried to escape, being wounded in the attempt: 'My husband has never tried to escape from jail, or even leave it under any pretext, including his health. Not having attempted to evade capture on 8 December, he does not want to prevent those responsible for his release from carrying out their duty.' This letter can and should be read as an attempt to prevent the shooting of her husband in jail, an action which would, of course, be covered up by the explanation that he had been trying to escape.

There were dark days ahead for Afonso Costa, as is testified by his prison writings. In one, he divided his acquaintances into *enemies*, *bad friends*, and *rare friends*. Of the second group – those who had turned their backs on him – he wrote *I want no greater suffering for them than the repugnance they must feel, in moments of lucidity, for their villainy.*[1] In a letter to his legal practice partner, Germano Martins, Costa lamented the sudden media attention on his finances: *What is the point of all of this, when no-one had found it odd that FIVE YEARS BEFORE THE REPUBLIC I already owned and ran an automobile to help me in my career, which was then at its pinnacle, since I had two offices, in Lisbon and Oporto, paying taxes in the highest bracket for both of them?*[2]

Unable to defend his good name, Afonso Costa discerned all around him the ruin of a lifetime's work; comparing himself with other disgraced politicians in Portuguese history, he found his situation to be the most lamentable of all: *I suppose that only* [the Marquis of] *Pombal had to face something similar to this, but, all the same, there was a trial at which he was present. Have we returned to the Jesuitical and Inquisitorial reaction of the mad Queen* Dona Maria I?[3] Costa's offices were raided by the new authorities, as was his safe-deposit box. Potentially damaging papers were released to the press. One aspect of Costa's private correspondence which suddenly made international headlines was the publication of a list of his enemies (along with an estimate of their net worth), which had been provided to Costa by pacifist financier Paul Bolo (better known as Bolo Pasha), in October 1916, during a dinner held in the home of French Senator Charles Humbert. This seemingly intimate contact with Frenchmen now facing accusations of treason was, unsurprisingly, exploited by his enemies. João Chagas called this 'one of the greatest indignities perpetrated by *Dezembrismo*'.[4] Eventually Afonso Costa was allowed to see his family, who shuttled to and from Elvas to keep his spirits up. At one point he began to write a biography, a project he never finished. As the weeks passed, his name appeared less and less frequently in the press. The wall of silence was finally broken by António José de Almeida in his newspaper *República*, on 9 March 1918: '[Afonso Costa] is more than just proscribed in his own country; he is dead to his own life. The bloodiest accusations and the most degrading insults have been levelled against him; waves of mud have crashed over him, covering his public life in rottenness and filth. But he is not allowed to speak […] It was not enough to take away his right to liberty; his right to moral existence – what is most respectable in the life of a man – has also been taken away. He was left with his physical existence but, it seems, as a favour.'[5]

On 30 March 1918 Afonso Costa was released. There then began a strange and secretive period, during which Costa remained in Portugal, but made no political utterances of any sort. He shied away from Lisbon, enjoying the hospitality of his future son-in-law's family;[6] he went on a boat trip near Aveiro; he requested leave from the Lisbon Faculty of Law, which was granted; and then, after a few more sightings around the country, he left, apparently without reason to do so. João Chagas, who had left the Paris legation in protest over the events in Lisbon, fumed, accusing Costa of cowardice, 'What is most shocking is his silence in the face of those who destroyed his power and attempted to dishonour him. It is as if his return to freedom is sufficient reparation'.[7]

Might a deal have been reached while he was in jail? While Sidónio Pais was alive, Afonso Costa did not stir, living a quiet life in Paris and resuming his existence as a lawyer. It seems, however, that this silence stemmed from the PRP's request for Costa to abstain from political activity, a necessary precondition for the overthrow of Pais's 'New Republic'. He had become a liability to his own party.

It is impossible to characterize the December 1917 coup which overthrew Afonso Costa's third and last cabinet as a mass movement. It was headed by Sidónio Pais, a Unionist politician, Minister of the Economy and then Finance in 1911–12 and, after that, Portugal's minister in Berlin. Like Costa, Sidónio Pais had been a lecturer in Coimbra (in Mathematics); unlike him, he had been a military officer as well. He had never brought too much attention on himself and, while in Berlin, Pais was kept largely out of the loop in terms of diplomatic decision-making. His party was willing to provide him, after his triumph, with some ministers (the most important of whom, Alberto de Moura Pinto, revised the law of separation of Church and State, Costa's great legislative triumph); but for added muscle he was forced to make a deal with the still imprisoned Machado Santos. Two factors aided his success. The first was that relations between the Democrats and the army had reached an all-time low, so that few of the senior officers still in Portugal were willing to move against the rebels, and many soldiers, slated for immediate departure to France, were willing to participate in Costa's overthrow. The second was that, in light of the constant strife in the capital since the start of the year, loyalty to the PRP, and the personal standing of its leaders, had been greatly eroded. For once, the civil revolutionaries stayed at home.

A recent biography of Sidónio Pais emphasizes his desire to return the Republic to its initial 'purity', to the very moment in which it triumphed over the monarchy and before the various political personalities began to abuse the regime for their own benefit. Its author also stresses Pais's desire to cooperate with the British in everything pertaining to the war, thus giving the lie to the many accusations, made during and after the war, that he was secretly in league with the Germans, who had imbued him with this task before he was sent home in March 1916.[8] While this is true, it is not the whole story. As we have seen, Portugal's belligerence, and its participation in the fighting, occurred, in many ways, against Great Britain's wishes. To follow London's lead was to curtail the CEP's independence, and to restrict its access to badly needed reinforcements, which is exactly what happened in 1918: no more soldiers were sent, officers coming home on leave were not made to return to France, and a reduction of the CEP's Front was agreed to, through the withdrawal of one division to the rear. There was a double gain to be made here – appeasing London (or at least the British military authorities) and earning the support of a war-weary population. Pais failed to rebuild the CEP after its destruction by the German army on 9 April 1918, and was unable to secure the military situation in Mozambique, where von Lettow-Vorbeck seemed able to move at will. For the interventionists, Sidónio Pais's war policy was both a betrayal and an abandonment of Portugal's high moral standing, jeopardising

Accused by his enemies of having been corrupted by the German government while stationed in Berlin as Portugal's minister, **Sidónio Pais (1872–1918)**, a mathematician by training, understood that he could earn the approbation of both the Portuguese population and the British government by limiting Portugal's involvement on the Western Front. He agreed to British proposals to restrict the Portuguese Front, and eventually to send the Portuguese Expeditionary Corps (CEP) to the rear, to rest. Pais also did little to send reinforcements from Portugal, or to rebuild the CEP after it had been destroyed during Operation *Georgette*, the German advance on 9 April 1918.

its chances at any future peace conference. In their view, Portugal had to give and give until the war was over, whatever the cost, overriding British objections if necessary.

More interesting, in many ways, was the high-wire act that Sidónio Pais had to perform while in power. He was a republican purist who was well liked by monarchists; opposed to political parties, he founded the Partido Nacional Republicano, which he hoped might attract all patriotic Portuguese, whatever their views. A man with an incredible hold over the crowd, especially in Lisbon, he was deserted, over the course of 1918, by the political elite, so that he was left with a cabinet of unknowns. An anti-clerical freemason, he reformed the law of separation and re-established diplomatic relations with the Holy See. His reform of the Senate brought in corporative representation; he ran unopposed for the presidency of the Republic and claimed an unlikely 500,000 votes; and without publishing a constitution he ushered in a presidential regime, concentrating power in his hands and transforming ministers into secretaries of state. Men who had been kicked out of the country by Afonso Costa for subversive actions, including the distribution of the *Rol da desonra*, were allowed to return to Portugal, publish newspapers and sit in parliament, to the consternation of Allied observers; a political police was created and well financed. Pais's style of governance provided a hint of things to come in southern Europe over the next decade: if not through his original intentions, then certainly through the compromises and U-turns he was forced to make in order to keep himself in power.

Sidónio Pais was barely able to celebrate the Allies' victory in November 1918. The previous month he had controlled a Democratic uprising; a week after the armistice, the UON declared a general strike against him. He responded with force, and two days after the strike had been broken organized a military display in Lisbon. But his days were numbered. The war over, monarchists, within and without the army, began to plan for his overthrow. This was the situation when ex-sergeant José Júlio da Costa shot him on 14 December 1918, in Lisbon's *Rossio* station. Journalist António Ferro, who would one day become Salazar's propaganda chief, would dedicate many an article to the murder of Sidónio Pais, and played on the coincidence of the surnames: 'Costa … the most repulsive, the most sordid element of that trinity of twins: Himself, the Costa who killed *Dom* Carlos, and the other one, who is in hiding abroad.'[9]

When the First World War came to an end, it was out of the question for Sidónio Pais to travel to Paris, given the tenuous nature of his hold on power. His choice of a representative was Egas Moniz. Moniz, a medical doctor of some renown (he would later share a Nobel Prize) whose political career had seemed over by 1911, was increasingly relied on by the hard-pressed Sidónio Pais to put out fires – he was named, in quick succession, parliamentary majority leader, minister in Madrid, and Foreign Secretary. It was in this capacity that Moniz set off for London early in December 1918 in order to confer with Arthur Balfour about the forthcoming negotiations; the two men met on 10 December.[10]

According to his own account of the meeting, Moniz laid out Portugal's objectives in the negotiations: the preservation and, if possible, expansion of the country's colonial territory, through a division of German East Africa; the resolution of Portugal's financial difficulties, notably its war-related debts to Great Britain, through a mix of reparations and a deal with London; and a share in war *matériel* seized from Germany, including a part of its fleet. Balfour was sympathetic, but non-committal. Sidónio Pais, though, was not best pleased, and belatedly sent his Foreign Secretary instructions regarding negotiations. Pais envisaged, in these last days of his life, a discrete Portuguese performance in the Paris negotiations, closely coordinated with the Foreign Office – a diplomatic performance matching his approach to the fighting on the Western Front. There could be no question of Portugal desiring more territory in Africa.

While still in London, Egas Moniz was informed of Sidónio Pais's murder, an event which was to launch Portugal into a period of great political turbulence. There is no doubt that this troubled state of affairs undermined the Portuguese delegation's actions in Paris, where Egas Moniz arrived on 20 December. With the country's attention fixed on its internal woes, and the settling of scores, little thought was spared for Moniz's mission, and indeed for the course of the peace negotiations. Moniz was further undermined by the actions of exiled republicans, notably Bernardino Machado and Afonso Costa, who used their contacts with the French press to denigrate Sidónio Pais and his followers.

The murder of Sidónio Pais released Costa from his political torpor. He viewed the murder in the same way he had viewed the 1908 regicide: *Part of our deepest woes have already received reparation thanks to an act which is perfectly explainable through recourse to collective psychology, and from which, as a result, no-one can distance himself, provided he was a part of the* [collective] *conscience which had formed itself. To* _want_ *or to* _oppose_ *such acts is pointless. They are like storms, with their electrical discharges. Of course, they have causes, they are determined, like all events in this universe. But the complexity, the size and the invincible strength of those causes make them inaccessible to men [...] This is* *all the more so since, before their outburst, everyone <u>feels and</u> <u>says</u> that they are coming.*[11]

The way forward, however, was not immediately clear; on 2 January 1919, Costa noted, in a brief diary entry, that *after dinner we considered various scenarios, all of which led to the conclusion that I cannot and must not return to domestic party politics.* He added, *it must be recognized that the biggest war, or, rather, the greatest efforts against my work came from inside …*[12] Still, Costa had discussed *my diplomatic, financial, economic and colonial plan*; his ambition had not vanished. The news gleaned from visitors recently arrived from Lisbon was not good. Sidónio Pais's funeral had revealed the scale of his popularity, while the Democrats were still despised by many, so much so that many senior party figures were now considering dissolving the party, creating a pan-republican organisation.

As soon as he arrived in Paris, Egas Moniz realized that, unlike London, he was now in unfriendly territory: 'The Government, especially Clemenceau, are very hostile.'[13] He cabled the Portuguese minister in London, asking for the British government to request its French counterpart to tone down press criticism of what was happening in Portugal. He would renew this request some weeks later, when he met Balfour in Paris.[14] At this time new instructions arrived from Lisbon, drafted by Sidónio Pais's successor, Admiral Canto e Castro. The new President, like his predecessor, stressed that Portugal must strive to cooperate with Great Britain in Paris, and insisted, in particular, on economic reparations: Portugal must be recompensed for its war effort and for the damage done by Germany, be it in Europe, the Atlantic islands, or, above all, in the colonies. It should also be indemnified for ships lost at sea and their cargo, and for property seized in

German territory. Missing from the list of objectives was any reference to territorial expansion.

After meeting Stéphen Pichon on 7 January, Moniz cabled home that French ill-will towards Portugal began at government level. The French Foreign Minister had been vague on all issues raised during the meeting, Pichon suggesting that the Portuguese cabinet contained men who had opposed the war. Moniz, not exactly noted for his interventionist sentiments during the conflict, lied: 'I replied that such an accusation was unfair. Portugal entered the war not because a political party so desired it, but because the whole country willed it.'[15]

One of the issues discussed at the meeting was that of Portugal's representation at the peace conference: how many delegates would it have? The issue was understood by all nations outside the five Great Powers (the US, Great Britain, France, Italy and Japan) as one of prestige – a pecking order of relevance. Early newspaper reports gave Belgium and Serbia three delegates but only two to Portugal. At a second meeting with Pichon, on 9 January, Moniz was assured that Portugal would have three delegates. On 14 January, however, a bombshell exploded: according to the Paris press, Portugal would be given a single representative, which placed it in the same rank as the countries which, despite declaring war on Germany, had not participated in the fighting. Egas Moniz and his collaborators blitzed the other delegations, large and small, reminding them of Portugal's material contribution to the Allied victory: 'In no case would it be admissible, that a country whose blood was shed together with that of the other Allies on the battlefield, should have the same representation as those nations who merely severed relations with the Central Empires without having sacrificed lives in the fight for the common cause.'[16]

Moniz was especially keen to meet with Balfour, given the nature of Anglo-Portuguese relations. He understood that, domestically, this demotion of the Portuguese delegation would have great repercussions, confirming interventionist denunciations of Sidónio Pais and his followers; he would stand or fall by his response to this emergency. He did not have long to wait. At the close of the very next day Balfour replied, 'I am very glad to inform Your Excellency that Portugal will be now represented by two delegates and will occupy a position similar to Belgium, a result which I trust Your Excellency will regard as eminently satisfactory.' [17]

No sooner was this victory achieved than Portugal fell into disarray, following a successful monarchist rising in the north of the country. The restoration of the monarchy was proclaimed in Oporto, and a governing junta established. To fight this danger, the remnants of the New Republic were forced to accept the collaboration of the men they had deposed. A coalition government, headed by José Relvas, was formed, in which Egas Moniz kept the Foreign Ministry. One of the priorities of this cabinet was to preserve the unity of republican opinion while the fighting was taking place. It was imperative that the republicans in exile in Paris did not stir and decide to return home. Augusto Soares and Germano Martins cabled Afonso Costa at the end of January, asking him to convince Bernardino Machado to remain silent until contacted by the government. [18]

It must be said that although the odds against them were considerable (they included delays in defining the mission's personnel, difficulty with payments and a lax approach by Lisbon in supplying the necessary information), Egas Moniz and the Portuguese delegation he headed in Paris rose to the challenge. In the face of French doubts about the Sidónio Pais regime and South African lust for Mozambican territory, the Portuguese scored a number of small victories, including election to two of the commissions set up by the Great Powers: the Commission for the League of Nations, and the Commission for Ports and Rail and Maritime Communications. A request was also made to form part of the Reparations Commission, and this was tenaciously repeated until Portugal was allowed in. Steps were taken to evaluate the scale of the financial losses suffered by the country (one provisional statement, presented to the Reparations Commission, put the total at £130,420,000, the biggest component being the £75,433,000 spent on actual military operations). Finally, markers were laid down in relation to Kionga, claimed for Portugal not out of desire for expansion but rather as rightful restitution, and a portion of the German battle fleet (3 light cruisers, 18 destroyers, 4 submarines, and a certain number of auxiliary vessels). All along, the Portuguese delegation sought to keep its British counterpart informed of its actions and intentions and reached out for British support whenever difficulties were encountered. The British delegation encouraged this level of cooperation. One area where help was actively sought was the colonial dimension of the Peace Conference, since South Africa's leaders, Louis Botha and Jan Smuts, openly acknowledged their expansionist ambition to the Portuguese representatives. They were willing to buy Mozambique, or to allow it to enter the Union with some degree of autonomy.

Ultimately, Egas Moniz's actions counted for little, given events in Lisbon. Having defeated the monarchist threat, republicans began to devour each other; given their greater strength, the 'old' republicans easily routed the leaderless 'new' republicans. On 22 February, after the final defeat of the monarchist insurgency, Sidónio Pais's parliament was brought to a close, since it did not reflect the new political reality of the land. On 26 February, a telegram was sent to Egas Moniz, informing him that the government had decided to widen his delegation, so as to include Afonso Costa and Norton de Matos, the most important figures in the interventionist pantheon. It was suggested that Egas Moniz might seek permission to widen the Portuguese representation to three delegates. Such a proposal was both absurd and insulting. Moniz replied two days later. While it was possible to increase the size of the delegation, it would be impossible to reopen the question of Portugal's representation at each meeting. He wrote that the government was free to add new names to the list of delegates but explained that the country's interests would be harmed by the replacement of those men who knew the workings of the various commissions, concluding, 'If my replacement is deemed to be advantageous, benefitting the foreign policy or even the domestic interests of the Government, my job will be entirely at your disposal [...] since the defence of the country's highest interests is my sole wish, my replacement would constitute the least of my sacrifices to the *Pátria*.' [19]

One of Portugal's delegates, the Count of Penha Garcia – who represented the country on the League of Nations Commission – now resigned. Egas Moniz did not go so easily, attempting to fight for his job. On 5 March, he registered a new success: Portugal was elected to the Financial Commission. Five days later, in a long telegram addressed to President Canto e Castro – the remaining political link to the Sidónio Pais regime – Egas Moniz listed his victories (the size of the delegation, membership of four commissions, preservation of the colonial empire and promise of Kionga's return, guarantee of the return to Portugal by the Allies of the German ships seized in 1916), explained the principles which guided him (the most important of which was cooperation with Britain, which he sensed was under threat, since some ministers wanted to align Portugal more closely with France) and asked the President to protect the Portuguese delegates to the conference, whose permanence in the French capital was deemed to be precarious.[20] This was, however, an unequal battle, and Egas Moniz's days in Paris were numbered.

5

Negotiating the Treaty, 1919

By late February 1919 it had become clear to all that Afonso Costa wanted Egas Moniz's job, and that, given Costa's incomparably greater political support base, there could be only one outcome. Even the deposed Prime Minister's rivals within his party were happy to keep him busy in Paris while they reinforced their position within the PRP. He made sure of their support on 3 March, when he wrote to the PRP's Directory, renouncing further involvement in party life. This was a combative statement of intent: Costa did not want to compete with other loyal republicans, but neither did he want to make deals with the 'new' republicans. Costa's note was one long 'I Told You So': *You do not ignore that, during the Provisional Government and, later, the Rua da Palma Congress, I always argued against the formation of different republican groupings while the Nation had not yet been set in motion by the impulse, and under the protection, of the new institutions; and that later, when I found myself at odds with the old companions from the heroic propaganda campaigns and the no-quarter fight against the monarchy, it was not because I intended to carry out, prematurely, a specialized programme that might be compared to other positive programmes, but because I was always implacable in the defence of the already conquered liberties and in the struggle against reactionaries of all sorts, and insensible to the doctrine of tolerance to, and recruitment of, the enemies of the Republic.*[1]

His warnings had been ignored; the 'New Republic' followed, with the result that in December 1917, *when my efforts with the Allies were finally crowned with complete success*, he and his family were insulted and humiliated in a way that not even the *biggest enemies of the Pátria* deserved. The party's response to this situation, *which would forever shame the country* if it were not dealt with, was to ignore him. He was turned into a pariah. Wanting to continue to serve Portugal and the Republic, Costa now felt that he must free himself from the constraints of party life. His one stated aim was to write a book detailing Portugal's participation in the conflict, *which will contribute to making more respected and esteemed our dear Republic, which the people love with such kindness and care.* The letter to the Directory was confidential; Alzira Costa informed her daughter, living in Lisbon, that when a suitable courier was found, a copy would be sent to her and her husband, Fernando de Castro: 'It is a good document; I am sure you will like it […] Your Father, who has worked so hard for the *Pátria* and the Republic, can do a lot for our dear country without being bound by a party, is that not the case?'[2]

On 2 March Jaime Leote do Rego, a leading interventionist who had commanded the Portuguese fleet until December 1917, returned to Lisbon from his Parisian exile. He engaged in a long series of meetings with political leaders. According to the *Diário de Notícias*, one subject under discussion was Portugal's representation abroad.[3] On 9 March, homage was paid to Leote do Rego in a Lisbon theatre. *O Século* was present, and summarised his speech: '[Leote do Rego] criticizes the achievements of *sidonismo*, which he claims was the work of treason and germanophilia, citing various facts to prove that treason and germanophilia – facts which cause the greatest excitement among the public which, finding it impossible to repress its rage, breaks out in protests and hostile cries against various diplomatic, military and political figures of the preceding political situation.'

The witch hunt had begun. It came as no surprise when, on 13 March, the *ad interim* Foreign Minister, Couceiro da Costa, informed Moniz that his mission in Paris had come to an end: there could be no co-existence of the Old and New Republics within the country's representation in Paris. Canto e Castro was powerless to help, explaining to Egas Moniz that the government had acted in accordance with domestic politics, and that he had no alternative but to accept the change.[4] On 17 March Moniz finally made way for Afonso Costa, who rebuilt the interventionist team around him, bringing in Augusto Soares and Norton de Matos. Costa would stress, in the coming months, how different the two delegations' approaches and priorities were. Indeed, with Costa at its head the Portuguese delegation's positioning and posturing changed considerably; but it is hard, looking back, to see how Portugal's prospects improved as a result of the change.

Afonso Costa's ambition was greater than that of his predecessor. He had a reputation to live up to, which demanded some striking success; and through that success, Costa hoped to redeem interventionist politics and revive his own career. As he put it to the new Prime Minister, on 1 April 1919,[5] *I hope with all my heart that your government will be able to rid the Republican State of all traitors to the* Pátria *and the enemies of our institutions.* He added that the Portuguese delegation would guide itself by these principles.[6] However, Afonso Costa arrived too late on the scene to have any significant influence over the shape and content of the Treaty of Versailles (with the exception of part of Article 298).

'All property, rights and interests of German nationals within the territory of any Allied or Associated Power and the net proceeds of their sale, liquidation or other dealing therewith may be charged by that Allied or Associated Power [...] with payment of claims growing out of acts committed by the German Government or by any German authorities since July 31, 1914, and before that Allied or Associated Power entered into the war. The amount of such claims may be assessed by an arbitrator appointed by Mr Gustave Ador [the Swiss President], if he is willing [...]'

ARTICLE 298, ANNEX, PARAGRAPH 4

Portugal was a small power and as such not consulted when the essential decisions were made; moreover, its military record had been dismal, notably in Africa (with the greatest disasters, notably the failure to contain von Lettow-Vorbeck, occurring under Costa's watch). What did change, however, was that the Portuguese delegation to the Peace Conference now became an unofficial Ministry for Foreign Affairs and, beyond this, an unofficial government. In addition to Soares and Norton de Matos, Costa summoned Teixeira Gomes and João Chagas, recently returned to the London and Paris legations they had manned during the war, to his team, and regularly cabled instructions to Lisbon, summoning experts and advisors to Paris and instructing the cabinet on what legislation needed to be introduced in order to back up his fictitious depiction of Portugal as a progressive country, socially advanced and colonially

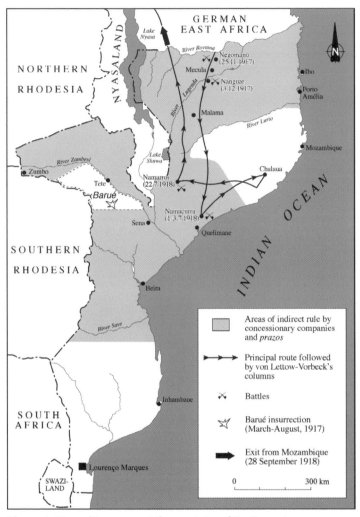

The war in Mozambique, 1917–18 (by permission of Jim Keenan)

PRESIDENT WILSON'S FOURTEEN POINTS, 8 JANUARY 1918

The program of the world's peace, therefore, is our program; and that program, the only possible program, as we see it, is this:

I. Open covenants of peace, openly arrived at, after which there shall be no private international understandings of any kind but diplomacy shall proceed always frankly and in the public view.

II. Absolute freedom of navigation upon the seas, outside territorial waters, alike in peace and in war, except as the seas may be closed in whole or in part by international action for the enforcement of international covenants.

III. The removal, so far as possible, of all economic barriers and the establishment of an equality of trade conditions among all the nations consenting to the peace and associating themselves for its maintenance.

IV. Adequate guarantees given and taken that national armaments will be reduced to the lowest point consistent with domestic safety.

V. A free, open-minded, and absolutely impartial adjustment of all colonial claims, based upon a strict observance of the principle that in determining all such questions of sovereignty the interests of the populations concerned must have equal weight with the equitable claims of the government whose title is to be determined.

VI. The evacuation of all Russian territory and such a settlement of all questions affecting Russia as will secure the best and freest cooperation of the other nations of the world in obtaining for her an unhampered and unembarrassed opportunity for the independent determination of her own political development and national policy and assure her of a sincere welcome into the society of free nations under institutions of her own choosing; and, more than a welcome, assistance also of every kind that she may need and may herself desire. The treatment accorded Russia by her sister nations in the months to come will be the acid test of their good will, of their comprehension of her needs as distinguished from their own interests, and of their intelligent and unselfish sympathy.

VII. Belgium, the whole world will agree, must be evacuated and restored, without any attempt to limit the sovereignty which she enjoys in common with all other free nations. No other single act will serve as this will serve to restore confidence among the nations in the laws which they have themselves set and determined for the government of their relations with one another. Without this healing act the whole structure and validity of international law is forever impaired.

VIII. All French territory should be freed and the invaded portions restored, and the wrong done to France by Prussia in 1871 in the matter of Alsace-Lorraine, which has unsettled the peace of the world for nearly fifty years, should be righted, in order that peace may once more be made secure in the interest of all.

IX. A readjustment of the frontiers of Italy should be effected along clearly recognizable lines of nationality.

X. The peoples of Austria-Hungary, whose place among the nations we wish to see safeguarded and assured, should be accorded the freest opportunity to autonomous development.

XI. Rumania, Serbia, and Montenegro should be evacuated; occupied territories restored; Serbia accorded free and secure access to the sea; and the relations of the several Balkan states to one another determined by friendly counsel along historically established lines of allegiance and nationality; and international guarantees of the political and economic independence and territorial integrity of the several Balkan states should be entered into.

XII. The Turkish portion of the present Ottoman Empire should be assured a secure sovereignty, but the other nationalities which are now under Turkish rule should be assured an undoubted security of life and an absolutely unmolested opportunity of autonomous development, and the Dardanelles should be permanently opened as a free passage to the ships and commerce of all nations under international guarantees.

XIII. An independent Polish state should be erected which should include the territories inhabited by indisputably Polish populations, which should be assured a free and secure access to the sea, and whose political and economic independence and territorial integrity should be guaranteed by international covenant.

XIV. A general association of nations must be formed under specific covenants for the purpose of affording mutual guarantees of political independence and territorial integrity to great and small states alike.

enlightened. This is all the more striking since Afonso Costa was an exception in Paris: he was neither a head of state nor a head of government; he was not even a foreign minister.

The vision of a new world order founded on peace, open diplomacy, collective security and generalized disarmament – the Wilsonian vision which determined so much of what was happening in Paris, as set out in his Fourteen Points of January 1918 – singularly failed to move the once radical Portuguese leader. Costa, it turned out, was more revanchist than even the French: his political career rested on the ability to win a 'good' peace for Portugal, one that might compensate it for its human and material sacrifices and therefore justify the interventionist position. At no stage did Costa believe that the establishment of the Wilsonian order sufficed as an end in itself. The League of Nations might allow a small country like Portugal to have greater international visibility – something which Portugal should take advantage of whenever possible – but it could not replace the punishment of Germany and the redistribution of its wealth as the most immediate Portuguese goals.

Egas Moniz, as we have seen, had assured Canto e Castro that the colonies were safe; Afonso Costa, three days after taking over the delegation, mentioned the South African pretensions to Portuguese territory as a *terrible danger, which of its own would justify our participation in the war*: all steps necessary to guard against this threat would be taken, but there simply had to be improvements in colonial administration.[7] In order to add weight to his defence of Portugal's colonial territories, Costa summoned to Paris Álvaro de Castro, Governor-General of Mozambique and one of the rivals for the leadership of the PRP. It was Castro who, with Freire de Andrade (a survivor from the Egas Moniz days), met Botha and Smuts on 21 April. Nothing had changed in the South

Africans' stance: It was Botha's belief that the interests of Mozambique would be best served by its entry into the South African Union, albeit with a large degree of autonomy: it might become, for example, a Dominion of South Africa, just as South Africa was a British Dominion. When told that the Lisbon government was intent on giving its colonies, especially Mozambique, much greater autonomy than had hitherto been the case, Botha replied that these were merely 'half-measures' that would satisfy no one.[8]

In response to this renewed manifestation of the South African threat, Costa now began to involve himself in domestic affairs, urging a reformulation of colonial arrangements through the creation of colonial High Commissioners – powerful officials capable of dealing independently with foreign governments: Álvaro de Castro in Mozambique and Norton de Matos in Angola. In a remarkable display of haughtiness, he wrote, *I will send [...] a projected decree to be published in accordance with Article 67 of the Constitution. The High Commissioners must be ready to leave in a few weeks' time without being dependent on a meeting of Parliament which will confirm the decree which creates those positions and assigns them their powers later, while the Senate will confirm the nominations.*[9] In other words, Costa, having identified the South African danger, wanted his conception of colonial administration to replace existing practice without parliamentary discussion, and wanted his nominees accepted without dissent. When events did not turn out as he wished them to, notably because of the delay in creating the new positions, his disappointment was intense.

One of Afonso Costa's first high-level meetings provides an important example of Afonso Costa's *modus operandi* in Paris and the gap between his expectations and the harsh reality. On 21 March, Costa met British Colonial Secretary Alfred Milner at the Hotel Majestic. The meeting was called by Milner, who explained that a special commission would probably be formed soon to take care of the distribution of mandates, and that he wanted to create consensus in advance of it meeting. Was Portugal interested in increasing its territory? Costa attempted to play a cagey game, explaining that, Kionga aside, he would have to wait to see what was on offer to the other Allies. Belgium was at the heart of the matter: if it received a mandate over an ex-German colony, then Portugal should be treated in at least similar terms. Milner was clearly not impressed, expressing the view that Portugal already possessed a large colonial territory. He went on to urge collaboration between Mozambique and South Africa, over which British influence was becoming negligible, and to inquire what steps Portugal was taking to establish why so many natives had helped the Germans during the war. Milner concluded by suggesting a territorial exchange between Portugal and Belgium, which desired the territory of Cabinda, on the west coast of Africa, in order to widen the Belgian Congo's access to the sea. Costa, understandably, refused; Milner likened his interlocutor's negative stance to that of Bismarck and suggested a more practical approach.

Upon taking office, Afonso Costa's priority had been to make himself known to the other delegations. Imbued as he was with the belief that the Allied Powers despised the New Republic and respected the interventionists, it was necessary to demonstrate to his interlocutors that the latter were back in the saddle. Meeting Balfour for the first time on 28 March, Costa immediately requested a seat on the forthcoming Executive Council of the League of Nations, explaining that Portugal's claim to such a privilege belonged in the moral sphere: it was a way for the Great Powers to recognize the altruistic nature of Portugal's intervention in the conflict. A similar place should be found for it on the Financial Commission, from which Portugal had been switched to the Economic Commission. Costa went on to defend what he believed to be Portugal's right to preferential status when it came to the payment of reparations; again, Portugal's 'moral' entitlement put it, he argued, in the first rank, since it had gone to war out of devotion to its ally and to elevated principles. To this was added the duty of the Great Powers to ensure that the small nations ruined by the conflict could rise again. Lastly, regarding territorial terms, Costa brought up Kionga and resurrected the matter of Olivença (now Olivenza, Spain), a border town seized by Spain in 1801 and never returned to Portugal despite a ruling to that effect by the Vienna Congress in 1815. Balfour showed little enthusiasm for any of Costa's demands, especially the last.

Similar requests were made to French Foreign Minister Pichon when the two men met on 30 March. Costa then played host to the Brazilian President, Epitácio Pessoa, on 15 April. A meeting with Woodrow Wilson left a good impression on Costa, the President having listened with apparent interest to Costa's presentation on *the reasons of a moral nature which took us to war* and his plea for membership of the Executive Council of the League of Nations. Costa took heart from Wilson's opinion that reparations should be distributed in accordance with each country's need and risk of ruin.[10] These high-level encounters would continue until the end of the Peace Conference, but with little result. In truth, little attention was paid to Costa's actions even by the Portuguese government; during March and April repeated entreaties had to be made for delivery of the delegates' formal letters of credentials. Costa considered the delay 'inexplicable' and warned that he might be prevented from signing the peace treaty if this state of affairs lasted much longer.

These tasks were largely self-imposed; but on 6 April Costa was reminded by telegram that the President, as well as the government, expected him to obtain a good result when it came to the re-equipping of the Portuguese fleet at Germany's expense.[11] The telegram was circulated to the press, which added to the pressure felt by the Portuguese delegation.[12] Costa was non-committal, adding that he would do his best to secure some of the vessels called for in the existing 'minimum programme' for the re-equipping of the fleet, adding, however, that he believed that most of the needed vessels should be purchased from Great Britain and the United States.[13] Nevertheless his talks continued, and France – the Great Power most interested in the division of the German fleet – was receptive to Portuguese arguments.

The weeks and months that followed saw the systematic defeat of Afonso Costa at the negotiating table; having raised the bar of Portuguese demands considerably, he was now unable to clear it. On 23 April a Portuguese representative was informed of the nature of the reparations arrangements so far worked out by the conference: an Inter-Allied Commission would determine, until 1 May 1921, the full extent of the reparations owed, which would be paid, in principle, until 1930 – or later, depending on Germany's economic state; reparations payments would be divided up among the Allies in accordance with percentages negotiated among themselves; military expenses were not to be included in reparations. This commission would be a small one, with voting representatives only from the Great Powers and Belgium, the other countries being represented by one non-voting delegate each. In order to kick-start economic activity in some countries, Germany would immediately pay 20 billion gold marks – but Portugal was not to be one of the recipients. Complaints from the Allied nations had to be presented quickly and in brief fashion.[14]

This was bad news, but worse was to follow. At the Plenary Session of 28 April the official announcement of Spain's entry to the Executive Council was made. Costa was livid: *The Portuguese delegation wishes to express its opposition to the naming by the Peace Conference of any neutral country as a member of the Executive Council of the League of Nations.*[15] Days later, at the 6 May plenary session, and fully informed of the dismay felt in Portugal over these reverses, Afonso Costa went on the offensive. He had suffered too many setbacks in the previous weeks not to react; he did so, playing the nationalist card to great effect. The terms to be presented to Germany, Costa announced, constituted an insult to Portugal and the other small countries represented around the table, both in their content and the way they had been arrived at. Portugal's financial losses were enormous, and potentially ruinous. Overall the conflict had cost the Portuguese economy some £225 million, somewhere between 37 and 47.5 per cent of the total Portuguese wealth – but, unlike other Allies, Portugal's territory and population would not be increased, making it harder for the State to recoup this investment through taxation. Should military expenses not be paid, as the Great Powers seemed to wish, the £80 million spent in fighting the war would be lost to the Portuguese economy.

What did Portugal ask for? *Given that no-one wanted to punish Germany like a criminal, she should at least pay us back, like a debtor, all that we had to spend to defend ourselves from her attacks [...] You say that Germany has no more money. And because you say that she has no more money, what lesson will be learned in the wake of the greatest crime ever committed since Humanity began? Will it be that in 1919, a country that committed four years' worth of crimes was not forced to pay even for the expenses of the monstrous conflict it provoked?*[16] Costa returned to the inclusion of Spain in the League of Nation's Executive Council: *Let us compare the small nations which threw themselves into the fire to defend the rule of Law and those that remained neutral. The Treaty ruins the former, and gives the latter both the advantage of profiting from the wealth amassed while others were sacrificing themselves and the honour of being a part of the first government of the League of Nations […] I request that my country, which sent its soldiers to France, be at the very least treated like those countries that sent only their travelling salesmen.*

The choice of Spain over Portugal fatally undermined one of the basic premises of the interventionist position which Costa personified: reinforcing, before the rest of the world, the distinction between republican Portugal and monarchist Spain, while presenting Portugal as the more progressive of the two countries in the Iberian Peninsula.[17] During the Plenary Session, the Portuguese delegation tabled a number of complaints: about the reparations payments, which did not include military expenses or the war's impact on international trade; about the division of reparations, which should prioritise the *small nations ruined by the war and who find it impossible to recover exclusively through their [own] efforts*; and about the Reparations Commission, where the Portuguese representative would not have a vote. Costa's complaints received some – but not much – notice abroad; domestically, the speech was lauded as a masterpiece, and as the telling of truths that needed to be heard. The very fact that it had been made, however, points to one inescapable conclusion: Portugal had been defeated at the negotiations in Paris.

Playing the nationalist card paid off in the short run. On 11 May Portugal's Foreign Minister informed Afonso Costa that public opinion had been shaken by the news that war expenses would not be covered by reparations, and that the government predicted public protests as a result. Should such protests be allowed – would they be of use to the Portuguese delegation – or should they be repressed?[18] Costa's reply was cautious. Journalists should be briefed individually and given access to diplomatic documentation, so that they might inform the public that *this matter was, and still is being, defended by this delegation with the greatest of energies.* As to the demonstrations, *They might have an excellent effect if inspired by pure patriotism, but the government should not forget that they might unexpectedly assume a grave character, given the persistence of damaging passions in Portuguese politics and the tendency of those with bad faith to exploit, for their profit, all events in public life.*

Less convincingly, Costa added that the country had to understand that it was collectively responsible for the final terms of the treaty, because of the international loss of face brought about by its domestic turmoil; it was also the case that other countries – Serbia, Romania, and even Belgium – were caught in the same bind.[19]

A few days later, and summarizing what had been achieved, Costa returned to his favourite theme: the contrast between Portugal's standing in 1919 and what it had been, thanks to his efforts, in December 1917: *It is sad but necessary to say that everything points towards the difficulty, even the impossibility, of restoring the admirable situation we had established in December 1917, during the last Allied Conference. It was a mere two months ago that we began the ascent of the* Via Dolorosa, *and there are spheres of action in which we cannot demonstrate the worth of our country.*[20]

Interventionist Portugal rallied to Afonso Costa's call, inundating the Hotel Campbell, where he was staying, with telegrams of congratulations for his defiance of the Great Powers on 6 May. Individuals, party commissions, municipalities, and selected associations demonstrated their faith in Costa's leadership. On 17 May, for example, the leadership of the Masonic order cabled: 'The Great Lusitanian Orient, interpreting the sentiments of the Freemasons and of the Portuguese people, rejoices in your attitude at the Peace Conference in favour of the justified rights of our *Pátria*, which gave the defence of justice and civilization not just the blood of its sons, but also the best part of its efforts.'[21]

What Afonso Costa understood, and what proved to be his (temporary) salvation, was that the treaty was not the final word on the post-war settlement. There was much still to be discussed, and plenty of opportunities to chip away at the edifice of the treaty. Wilson might well object to the inclusion of war expenses, but the other Allies were not going to let the matter drop, since *Serbia, for example, would need a sum greater than its old budget just to pay the interest on the debts generated by its war expenses*. Costa sought also to demonstrate to the Portuguese government that while his ideas had been defeated, they had nevertheless been appreciated by the other delegations, even those of the Great Powers.[22] The government was not in a position to question this judgement; on 23 June a telegram transmitted its fulsome praise to the head of the Portuguese delegation. Portugal might not have been treated with due justice in Paris, but it had to pay its respects to the 'great citizen' who had deployed, on its behalf, his 'exceptional qualities of intelligence, hard work, patriotism and rare talent'.[23]

6
Domestic Reaction and Ratification, 1919–1920

The Treaty of Versailles was signed on 28 June 1919. Admiral Canto e Castro expressed the hope that the event would mark a new start for Portugal and for the Republic, to be brought about by the effort and the union of all Portuguese.[1] This, of course, was optimistic. Portuguese commentators, like others around the world, found it hard to grapple with a treaty so far removed from their immediate concerns. For Afonso Costa, however, there was still much to negotiate. His mission was by no means finished, but for it to continue the Congress had to ratify the Treaty.

One issue that was still ongoing was that of naval re-equipment. On 3 June, Costa had sent the Secretary-General of the Peace Conference an official request for the vessels, to be distributed by the members of the Supreme Council. As before, the bar was set high: four light cruisers, twelve destroyers, four submarines, and an unspecified number of smaller craft. The document stressed the defensive ends to which such warships would be put. Little was heard on the matter until December, when Foreign Minister João Carlos de Melo

Barreto asked for concrete information. *O Século*, he pointed out, had reported that Portugal would be allotted the equivalent of the auxiliary vessel *Augusto Castilho*, sunk by submarine ace Lothar von Arnauld de la Perière in October 1918, and a number of small craft for colonial duties. This bore little relation to the earlier Portuguese requests, and Melo Barreto would surely be questioned on the matter in parliament.[2] On 9 December, however, the Great Powers handed down their verdict on the German fleet: what remained of it was to be destroyed, with the exception of nine cruisers, five of which would go to France and four of which would go to Italy. There was still some hope that Portugal might be given a gunboat and some smaller vessels.[3] That same day, Melo Barreto forwarded a request from the Ministry of the Navy for a dredger and a floating dock capable of handling ships up to 2,000 tons. On 10 December, Portugal was finally informed that it would receive a gunboat, to be used in whatever way it saw fit, and six torpedo boats which, having been stripped of their primary weapons, might be used for policing duties.[4] Although this fell short of expectations, Melo Barreto cabled his and the Navy Minister's satisfaction; he also informed the Senate of the reparation.

In April of the following year, however, it became clear that the longed-for dredger and floating dock would not come to Portugal. Costa was furious to see even this minor request turned down: […] *once again, the so-called Great Powers disposed with complete sovereignty of war* matériel, *on land and on sea, be it to have it scrapped, be it to have it distributed, with rare exceptions, […] as if only they had been in the war and only they should be prepared to defend Law and Civilization in the case of another war!*[5] This was not the end of this largely unhappy chapter. On 7 May 1920 Teixeira

Gomes, Portuguese minister in London, informed Costa that the promised gunboat was Turkish and the de-fanged torpedo boats Austrian. These were in fact 'Type F' boats, with a crew of 38 and a displacement of 266 tons. Similar vessels were distributed to Romania and Greece. Unfortunately for Portugal, two of these ships broke free from the ship towing them to Portugal during a storm and were lost. The Turkish warship never materialised.

As we will see in the next chapter, other matters weighed more heavily on Afonso Costa than the navy's fate, and for these to be resolved he needed to convince his countrymen to accept a treaty he himself had decried as manifestly unfair. On 1 July 1919 a prescient Costa warned that the most urgent problem facing Portugal was the ratification of the Treaty of Versailles. Once again, he pointed the way forward: a special commission of the Chamber of Deputies, with representatives of all parties, had to be constituted to analyse the text of the treaty, which should be translated as soon as possible.[6] It was imperative, Costa understood, to ratify the treaty before its grey areas began to be better defined, and its revision was attempted by countries which were quicker off the mark. This, of course, was linked to Costa's understanding that there was still much to play for, the treaty not being the final word on all matters of interest to Portugal. Not for the first time, though, Afonso Costa's desire for quick action – one might even say for the suspension of all critical thought by Portugal's legislators, to be sacrificed on the altar of national interest as defined by Costa – crashed headlong into the twin obstacles of political instability and anti-interventionist sentiment, whose proponents were still holding out for a full and frank debate on why Portugal had gone to war. Their leaders, beginning with Brito Camacho, knew much of the content of the negotiations between London and Lisbon; Brito Camacho, after all, had been briefed in the run-up to war by Bernardino Machado, and Portuguese governments were anything but watertight. For the war's opponents, a new battleground was found in the shape of the *White Book*, which brought together diplomatic documents on Portugal's intervention in the conflict, from start to finish. Such a publication had become a political necessity dictated by the post-Sidónio Pais rapprochement between republicans of all hues – the trend to which, as we have seen, Afonso Costa objected.

Aware as they were of the difficulties involved in bringing Portugal into the war, opposition figures such as Brito Camacho never stopped calling for the publication of a *White Book* on the country's handling of the crisis. Only the first part of the *White Book*, detailing events prior to the German declaration of war, was published in 1920 after the ratification of the Treaty of Versailles, and the documents it contained suffered important cuts. Missing, for example, was a Spanish offer of joint action in relation to the German merchant ships, which made possible a peaceful alternative to their seizure.

On 11 August, Foreign Minister Melo Barreto, who regularly reaffirmed his desire to follow Costa's advice on all matters pertaining to the Peace Conference, informed Costa that despite the steps already taken – a plan for the two chambers to elect a commission for the study of the treaty, and the distribution of copies of the document in French – there was no immediate prospect of its ratification. Time had been spent in the election of a new president of the Republic – António José de Almeida – and the Congress was about to close for its summer holiday. Unless the government called a special session in September, ratification would be delayed until the reconvening of parliament in October.[7] Costa saw no need to hurry the process along at this stage; however, he would soon change his mind.

Some in Portugal did not understand the continued exist-
ence of its delegation in Paris after the signing of the treaty.
Senator Afonso de Lemos, a republican veteran, asked Melo
Barreto on 19 August when Costa's work would be finished,
since the end of the delegation's work would bring an important saving for the country's finances. This allowed the Foreign
Minister to launch into a long defence of Costa's actions in
Paris, whose end could not yet be estimated. On 21 October,
Costa suggested that with the coming signing of the peace
treaty with Bulgaria – at the end of the month – his mission
might be coming to an end. After that, he would write his
final report and bring the delegation's work to a close. This
did not occur, however, although the delegation was reduced
in size – not always with the agreement of its members – and
Costa came to rely more and more on Teixeira Gomes and
João Chagas.

In another demonstration of the limits of Afonso Costa's
authority, constituting a viable delegation for the Washington International Labour Conference in October 1919 proved
difficult. Afonso Costa had originally stated his willingness
to go to America provided there was no pressing matter in
Paris, but quickly changed his mind, preferring instead to
continue in France. One after another his candidates for the
Washington mission declared their unwillingness to participate. Norton de Matos was Costa's immediate choice as his
replacement; when he refused, despite Costa's direct entreaties, the choice moved on to Augusto Soares. It did not stop
there; Melo Barreto wrote, on 14 October, that five men had
now turned down his invitations. Some days later, he would
lament the 'stubbornness' displayed by those who declined
to represent their country at such an important gathering.
Even finding berths for the delegation, at the last minute,

proved hazardous. Costa was deeply frustrated; the United States Embassy in London had promised to provide transport, and then had washed its hands of the affair – but it was crucial for Portugal to be present, so that it might show *the immense progress made by republican legislation in favour of workers.*[8]

On 22 October Afonso Costa wrote that the time had come to do something about ratification. Once the treaty came into operation, its signatories would have rights and responsibilities, but only those who had ratified it would be able to pursue their interests actively. This was true, for example, when it came to pressing Portuguese claims for all kinds of reparations, as well as in moving towards the creation of the tribunal called for in paragraph 4 of Article 298.[9] Melo Barreto was confident that the matter would soon be resolved; everything was ready, he wrote, for the Congress to discuss the treaty and ratify it in the first fortnight of November. Despite these assurances, time dragged on with no action taken, so that on 17 December Costa returned to the topic: the treaty would soon come into effect – it would then become *inexplicable and in many ways inconvenient* for Portugal not to follow suit. He asked Melo Barreto for a precise date when ratification might occur.[10] Melo Barreto replied that discussion of the treaty would begin after the Christmas holidays, his estimate being that the affair would be concluded by the second fortnight of January.[11] On 5 January Afonso Costa, reminding Melo Barreto of what was at stake – he could only initiate the proceedings outlined in Article 298 once Portugal had ratified the treaty – called ratification an *imperious patriotic duty.*[12] No one else really regarded it as such; on 8 January 1920 he was informed that the government presided over by Alfredo Sá Cardoso, an army officer with impeccable republican credentials, had fallen as a result of disagreements in parliament over how best to deal with the country's mounting financial crisis.[13] The following day Melo Barreto assured Costa that he would impress upon his successor as Foreign Minister the importance of the ratification procedure, adding that the drive for ratification had met with some opposition from elements who demanded that it be accompanied by a discussion of Portugal's intervention in the conflict, on the basis of the *White Book*.

On 12 January, as the political vacuum dragged on, Melo Barreto maintained that the question of ratification would be dealt with before the month was out. But nothing seemed to work when it came to resolving the political crisis. When António José de Almeida's attempts to form a national government were thwarted by the disagreements within the PRP, he turned to the Liberal Party – an unstable fusion of the old Evolutionists and Unionists – to form a cabinet.[14] Costa was not pleased; just as ratification was high on the agenda, some of his old Unionist foes would enter government! He was not alone, however, in opposing this new set of circumstances. A large and belligerent crowd marched on the Terreiro do Paço, making it clear that it would not tolerate a cabinet which contained members who had not opposed, or who had actually collaborated with, Sidónio Pais. Fernandes Costa, the putative Prime Minister, immediately halted his attempts to form a cabinet, and the ball bounced back to the Democrats. This time, the President's desire for a strong government of republican reconciliation seems to have been listened to; Domingos Pereira, of the PRP, headed a cabinet which included Democrats, Liberals and Socialists. Melo Barreto was retained as Foreign Minister, which was good news for Afonso Costa.

Given the new circumstances, Costa believed the time had

come to act on the matter of ratification once and for all: *All parliamentary discussion about participation in the war and the peace terms could be carried out quickly, there being solemn declarations by the various leaders and a promise of a wider debate on the occasion of the presentation of the* White Book *or the report by the Peace Delegation. No-one needs to cover up what happened in relation to this most important event in Portuguese history, or can hope to gain from such an action, but we must all bring to an end the ambiguous situation in which the delay in ratifying the Treaty places us.*[15] Costa, eager to impart to Lisbon the importance of acting, went further, threatening to resign if the matter were not dealt with swiftly.

A week later Costa was informed by Melo Barreto that the bill for the approval of the treaty had been presented to the Chamber of Deputies, and that he, Melo Barreto, had spoken on the subject for an hour. The bill had been well received, the Foreign Minister explained, and Afonso Costa's name had been loudly hailed as the 'glory of the Republic, symbolizing the campaign in defence of our rights in this decisive phase'.[16] The presentation of the bill did not mean, however, its immediate ratification. More than a fortnight later the Portuguese delegation received a letter from the Reparations Commission, informing it that when affairs affecting Portugal were discussed, the commission would invite a Portuguese representative to participate in the deliberations – provided the country had ratified the treaty. Should ratification not have been carried out, the Portuguese representative's powers would be restricted. Costa reacted predictably, informing Melo Barreto that one of his fears had just materialized: Portugal's desire to participate constructively in the commission's committees was becoming increasingly unrealisable.[17]

Melo Barreto could only apologize and express the hope that the new president of the commission, former French President Raymond Poincaré, would continue to be well disposed towards Portugal, cancelling out the effects of non-ratification. Afonso Costa insisted on moving towards ratification quickly; Teixeira Gomes had met Gustave Ador, who had shown his willingness to name an arbitrator to resolve the dispute with Germany, once invited to do so by the Supreme Council – but this, of course, could only happen if the treaty was ratified.[18] The same point was repeated in a different telegram sent the same day, this time dealing with the sharing out among the Allies of Germany's merchant marine – be it those ships already in Allied hands (such as the ones seized by Portugal in 1916), or those Germany had agreed to provide under Article 244 of the treaty.

The Portuguese delegation was employing all channels of communication to assert Portugal's rights, but, as Afonso Costa emphasized to his Foreign Minister, since it could not act officially, it was hamstrung in its action: *I believe it for my part indispensable for parliament to state whether or not it wants to delay, for whatever pretext, a ratification on which so much – the protection of our most important rights and interests, resulting from the participation in the war – depends, since the responsibilities which the government and the Portuguese delegation are amassing – the former through its inaction and the latter through its presence here – seem to me to be extremely grave.*[19]

Given Portugal's political instability, and the resulting and constant changes of government, it was impossible to predict when any piece of legislation might emerge from the Congress. A wave of strikes swept across Portugal, affecting railway workers, postal and telegraph staff, and civil servants.

Domingos Pereira's government resigned; another one, led by Democratic strongman António Maria da Silva, seemed ready to take its place. This cabinet was never to take shape; instead, Álvaro de Castro, who had by now broken with the imploding PRP, was invited to form a government, but he too failed in this increasingly difficult task.

Afonso Costa's patience was wearing thin when, on 10 March, he was informed that António Maria Baptista was trying to form a government that would include, as Foreign Minister, and not for the first time, Rodolfo Xavier da Silva. The days passed and there was no news; on 16 March Costa complained that he had received no word from Lisbon since the fall of the Domingos Pereira cabinet; worse still, official press releases announced that parliament had postponed its sessions; this meant, he added, that *the urgent necessity of the ratification of the Peace Treaty has not yet been felt there.* All hope of an active part in the search for justice on the reparations front was for the time being frozen.

The situation was intolerable for the Portuguese delegation: *In the light of Parliament's postponement and the attitude so far adopted by the government in relation to the ratification of the Peace Treaty, Portuguese delegates Vitorino Guimarães and Barbosa de Magalhães* [in Paris as financial advisors to Afonso Costa] *leave today for Lisbon, desiring to represent Portugal only when they can do so officially, all the more [so] since we have been informed that, for as long as the present situation lasts, it is only with me, as President of the Portuguese Delegation, or with my substitute or representative, that the matters of interest to our country might be handled* [...][20] In the meantime, Costa concluded, he would hang on, working to prevent Portugal from being completely forgotten in this final phase of the Peace Conference.

Costa had already gambled – he himself admitted as much – by informing Poincaré that ratification would be completed by Easter. Given the positive nature of his conversation with the President of the Reparations Commission, Costa now begged the government to act; this opportunity should not be lost. In the meantime, however, the proofs of the *White Book* which had been sent from Lisbon to Afonso Costa by registered post went missing, which was unsurprising given the scale and nature of the industrial action taking place in Portugal. Then, out of the blue, on 25 March Costa was informed by the Foreign Minister that the Congress had been summoned to an extraordinary sitting, for 30 March, in order to ratify the treaty. For once the government held to its promise, and the session went ahead as planned. The parliamentary commission which examined the document found it to be, despite obvious shortcomings, 'worthy of our respect', and recommended its approval.[21]

Debate was limited, with Brito Camacho, as expected, and Ramado Curto, a Socialist deputy, speaking against the treaty. The former Unionist leader had so many targets at which he was aiming that the impact of his words was defused, and he failed to deliver a telling blow. There was as yet no *White Book*, he argued; no report by Afonso Costa on his action; no way of evaluating his performance. Costa had resigned his mandate as deputy, and did not feel the need to explain his actions to the Congress; the Congress meekly allowed him to do so: 'We are the sole country whose delegation to the Peace Conference is presided over by someone who allowed himself to turn his back on parliament, foregoing the undeniable duty of justifying his actions before it, and deriving from his contact with parliament the strength necessary to impose his demands.'[22] Camacho noted also that the Netherlands, although neutral, had preserved its empire, while Denmark, also neutral, had seen its territory grow. Despite these cutting remarks, an almost unanimous approval of the bill was given the following day. The republican press weighed in behind Costa's desire on this front, *O Mundo* declaring that parliament should not harm the country by engaging in pointless and sterile discussions: it was in no position to add to the constructive criticism of the Treaty, and it should not turn the issue into a party political conflict.[23]

On 1 April – and it was no April Fool's prank – Xavier Silva at last informed Afonso Costa that the Treaty of Versailles had been approved by the Portuguese Congress. Little had been added in the discussion, except for a call for a report from Costa on his delegation's action in Paris. *O Mundo* attacked even this call: reports should be written only when a mission had been concluded, and Costa's was not yet finished. 'The *aria* of the *White Book* having finished, it is replaced by the *aria* of the report! All that is needed is a pretext to attack!'[24]

No such report ever materialized. On 3 April, however, the Foreign Minister's *Chef de Cabinet* departed for Paris, carrying with him the formal letter of ratification by the Congress of the Treaty of Versailles.

Afonso Costa of Portugal, the newly elected President of the League of Nations photographed in Geneva. 11 March 1926

III

The Legacy

7
Undoing the Treaty, 1920–1921

As seen in the previous chapter, ratification of the Treaty of Versailles by the Portuguese Congress took longer than expected, leaving Afonso Costa exasperated. Well before ratification, however – before even the treaty had been signed – Costa had begun to attempt to revise some of its aspects, and to shape, in Portugal's favour, the responses to questions left unanswered by the treaty's many articles. The two most important areas were the defence of Portugal's empire and financial reparations.

One of the most worrying aspects of the treaty, as far as Afonso Costa was concerned, was the change of approach towards colonization that it embodied. Portuguese colonization alternated between brutality and wishful thinking. The empire, made up of two territories too large for Portugal to occupy and develop and the scattered remnants of former glories, made little geographical sense, and, with a few exceptions, could only be kept by force. Wartime events had revealed how precarious the Portuguese hold over Angola and Mozambique was; yet all colonial powers were now deemed to have very real obligations towards their colonial subjects, moving beyond simple pacification and towards actual improvements in quality of life.

Costa, a jurist, saw the reformulation of Portugal's colonial administration and the introduction of the High Commissioners as key to buying time for Portugal. On 13 May 1919 he had met Alfred Milner and, mistakenly, thought him better disposed towards Portugal's pretensions in Africa.[1] The following day Costa submitted a note to the Supreme Council stating that *Portugal, by its unforgettable services to Humanity and Civilization, especially in the African continent, which it has been watering with its blood since the 14th century, and by its direct and indirect sacrifices during this War, believes itself entitled to receive from the Peace Conference a treatment which is at least equal to that which might be meted out to any other power which followed it in the work of colonizing Africa.*

When *Le Temps*, on 6 June 1919, cast doubts on Portugal's colonizing ability, Costa had responded immediately, writing, in a letter published on 9 June, that *the fact that Portugal needs financial help in order to carry out the development of its colonies does not demonstrate that its people do not possess colonizing qualities.* Costa was not giving up on the possibility of a mandate. Meeting Milner again, in London on 12 July 1919, in the context of the recently constituted Special Commission on Colonial Mandates, he had repeated his view that everything hinged on Belgium's treatment by the conference: should it receive a mandate, Portugal's prestige would demand that it too be given one. Milner had remained unimpressed – was it not the case that Portugal had financial difficulties in relation to Mozambique? If part of German East Africa were handed to Portugal as a mandate, would Portugal accept turning the whole of Mozambique into a mandate? And what of the complaints about Portuguese treatment of the 'native races'? Costa had countered these points, not entirely convincingly, by casting doubt on the reliability of evidence from anti-colonial critics like the late Sir Roger Casement or the radical E.D. Morel, whom he described as *enemies at the same time both of Portugal and England.*[2]

On 25 September, the Supreme Council of the Allied and Associated Powers had recognized Portugal's claim to ownership of the Kionga triangle. Costa then embarked on a long piece of subterfuge, claiming the attribution of Kionga as a major victory while burying the fact that Belgium had been given a mandate over Rwanda and Burundi. In a long letter dated 27 September 1919, addressed to Melo Barreto, Costa went over the negotiations in relation to mandates, the future of Mozambique and Kionga; he stressed how difficult it had been to interest men like Milner and Balfour in the issue, and how ill disposed they had been towards Portugal at the start of the negotiating process. Once again he set up his favourite comparison: *A heroic effort was called for in order to return to the prestigious position that we had reached in the Allied countries as a result of our participation in the war, as demonstrated by the warm and enthusiastic reception afforded to the Head of State of the Portuguese Republic in France, England and Belgium in October 1917 and in the concessions made to the Portuguese plenipotentiaries during the Allied Conference of November of the same year.*[3]

The full extent of the harm caused by Sidónio Pais had been demonstrated, Costa continued, by a message delivered on 9 April on behalf of Balfour, which had effectively blocked the return of Kionga unless certain British concerns about the treatment of the indigenous population were addressed.

Costa, while complaining about a lack of order in Portugal, both in the spirit of men and on the streets, and about the failure to deliver on the High Commissioners, also dealt at length with the 12 July meeting with Milner's commission in London, quoting at length from its minutes. He did so for a simple reason, contained in one passage: *That was the London meeting. Afterwards, and fearing that there would be an insistence on attributing us the Kionga Triangle as a mandate, which would represent a total humiliation for Portugal, we stopped at nothing to ensure that the decision was favourable to us.* In other words, Costa retroactively moved the goal-posts. Initially his priority had been to ensure that Portugal was given a mandate should Belgium get one too; now, for the first time, he informed Lisbon that his priority had been to secure Kionga as an act of justice, and not as a mandate. 'Total humiliation' had thus been averted, but he said nothing about Belgium's significant triumph in securing a mandate over Rwanda and Burundi.

The prevailing impression one gets from the documentation is that the British did not care about Kionga – in truth, the Portuguese did not care very much for it either – and could not see what all the fuss was about. Costa closed his letter with a very negative description of the new colonial order. Where once the powerful nations had used brute force to get their way in Africa, they had now created a set of institutions – the League of Nations and the International Labour Organization (ILO) – through which they could covertly assert their expansionist claims in the colonial sphere. In the articles the Treaty of Versailles dedicated to the welfare of the colonial peoples, and in the principles guiding the ILO, Costa claimed to discern only a trap for smaller colonizers such as Portugal, for whom the world had become a more dangerous place.

On 27 September 1919 *O Mundo*, reacting to the news from Paris, stated that 'the fact of Kionga's recovery is sufficient of itself to justify our intervention in the war, where Portuguese virtues were so eloquently demonstrated'. This, of course, was, at best, empty rhetoric, at worst idiocy: Kionga was intrinsically worthless. Costa's prompting eventually led to seemingly significant changes in colonial administration. In August 1920, after some delay, the Congress approved a law outlining a process of devolution of power to the colonies, in accordance with each one's development, and allowing for the naming of High Commissioners, as Costa had long advocated. Norton de Matos was named as Angola's High Commissioner, as Costa had wished; disappointingly for Costa, Brito Camacho, rather than Álvaro de Castro, was appointed to the Mozambique job. The practical results of this would prove, however, negligible.

Afonso Costa's hopes in relation to the positive impact of High Commissioners on Angola and Mozambique would be dashed in the 1920s. In Mozambique, Brito Camacho found himself essentially powerless, since much of the territory was still controlled by foreign-owned concessionary companies and South African mines acted as an important source of paid employment for Mozambicans. In Angola, Norton de Matos enjoyed greater authority, and attempted to fast-track the material transformation of the colony (as well as, contradictorily, fomenting immigration and abolishing labour impositions on Africans), only to be defeated by financial difficulties and the opposition of the white population.

Although hampered by parliament's slowness to ratify the Treaty of Versailles, Afonso Costa did not stop trying to act on the reparations front; for him, as for almost all other delegations, this was the most important area of dispute in the wake of the treaty's signature. On 28 January 1920 he wrote to Sir John Bradbury, Britain's representative on the Reparations Commission, asking if Portugal might be awarded representation on some of the committees to be set up by the commission. His own preference was for the committees on shipping and on cables. Bradbury replied that he would alert the chairman of the Reparations Commission to this request.[4]

In 1920, Raymond Poincaré's appointment as president of the Reparations Commission was generally well received by the Portuguese, since he was understood to be keen to impose a harsh settlement on Germany. Costa met Poincaré on 18 March in the Hotel Astoria, and was told that it was Poincaré's intention to reverse the serious errors made during the Peace Conference. His words were music to Afonso Costa's ears. According to Poincaré, while it was the Allies' responsibility to promote the economic recovery of the enemy nations, it was their greater duty to ensure that all peoples who had sacrificed themselves for law and justice should be helped. Portugal, Belgium and Romania, 'Latin nations' all, were especially dear to France, and he would do his utmost to pursue their interests. Such words, wrote Costa, were said *with a passion and an enthusiasm that are not common in him.*

Costa had a long agenda for this meeting. He renewed requests for the Portuguese delegate to have a vote in the commission and for Portuguese participation in the committees, only for Poincaré to inform him that the commission had recently ruled against this. According to his account of the meeting, Costa attacked this decision with such vehemence that Poincaré, *visibly impressed*, announced that he would take the matter back to the Commission. Costa did not end there; he renewed, in melodramatic terms (*my patriot's heart still bleeds from the open wound*) the complaint about Spain's invitation to the Executive Council of the League of Nations and brought up the matter of Article 237. Portugal's war expenses, he explained, amounted to more than £80 million, while the economic losses to Portugal were now thought to have been in the region of £240 million. Given that Article 237 called for reparations to be shared out according to the principle of equitability, and according to the rights of each country, should it not be the case that countries facing hardship, such as Portugal, should receive priority in that sharing out? He had already called for such special treatment during the negotiations, to no avail; Article 237, however, might be interpreted in this light, allowing Portugal a sort of preference and allotting it a fixed percentage of Germany's first reparations payments. Poincaré renewed his good wishes towards Portugal, but promised nothing concrete.

Finally, Costa asked Poincaré if compensation to Portugal for the damages caused by Germany before 1916 was to be received via the commission, or through some other channel. Poincaré confessed to knowing little about the issue, *perhaps because Portugal was one of the few allied countries that benefited from paragraph 4 of the Annex to Article 298*; in any case he thought little could be done on this matter until the treaty had been ratified by Portugal. This was a sign of difficulties to come. As Costa made his way out, he asked Poincaré *not to forget Portugal and to act always as its defender, with his head and his heart*; Portugal deserved this, since *its soldiers had also placed their heart and intelligence in the defence of invaded and martyred France's sacred soil.*[5]

On 7 April, in the wake of Portugal's ratification of the Treaty of Versailles, Costa again met Poincaré, to inquire as to the best way of pursuing Portuguese interests regarding reparations in general and certain issues in particular – Portugal's share both in the division of Germany's merchant fleet and of financial reparations. The exact manner in which division of the latter would be arrived at had not yet been decided, but it seemed that a conference might be organized to discuss a solution.

The ratification of the treaty also allowed Costa to move swiftly to set up the arbitration tribunal into events in Africa before 1916. This meant contacting former Swiss President Gustave Ador and inviting him to name an arbitrator. On 8 April, the Portuguese minister in Switzerland cabled Ador, asking to be received. At the same time, however, Costa invited the Conference of Ambassadors, one of the Peace Conference's highest decision-making bodies, to convey an official Portuguese request for Ador to nominate an arbitrator; Costa foresaw no difficulty.[6] Ador acceded to the Portuguese diplomat's request, warning, however, that those he thought fit to invite might not accept, and asking for clarification on their payment. He nevertheless settled on Alöis de Meuron, an experienced jurist and a member of Switzerland's National Council. De Meuron was described by the Portuguese minister as 'excessively Francophile', a very talented lawyer and an influential liberal politician. Costa, understandably, was pleased.

In London, Teixeira Gomes impressed on the Foreign Office the need for the Conference of Ambassadors formally to invite Ador to nominate an arbitrator. While Lord Derby was instructed to 'support Portuguese claim and if Conference takes contrary view you should urge that Portuguese Delegate be heard before decision is arrived at', unfortunately the Conference of Ambassadors refused to become involved in the issue, judging it a matter for the Portuguese government.[7] What this meant, in practice, was that the Great Powers were distancing themselves from any claim Portugal might make against Germany under this little-known provision of the treaty.

Costa complained to Teixeira Gomes that, *In this manner the Conference of Ambassadors does not interest itself in the execution of the Treaty* […] *The Conference goes further: it tells an Allied Nation, which is demanding the constitution of a court of arbitration designed to sit in judgement of her claims against Germany, that it has nothing to do with the matter, and that she must look after herself, trying to have an arbitrator named as per the Treaty!*[8] The Conference of Ambassadors was either negligent or intent on reducing Portugal's rights, Costa insisted, and he urged Gomes to make his protest heard in the Foreign Office, since, if nothing else, Lord Derby had not followed London's instructions, allowing the matter to be dropped by the Conference of Ambassadors against Portugal's wishes without having Afonso Costa heard.

It was decided at the San Remo conference, held in April 1920, that the Allied powers would establish the sum total of the reparations owed by Germany earlier than allowed for in the treaty. Costa, who had at first disbelieved the rumours to this effect, urged Lisbon to hurry the process of establishing the complete Portuguese reparations bill, in order to present it to the Allies when necessary.[9] While this preparation was taking place, a new source of worries opened up for Costa. The British government began to insist on the prompt repayment of its wartime loans to Portugal. Wartime arrangements stated that such loans would be repaid two years after the signing of a putative peace treaty; such a treaty had been signed in June 1919, so the loans should therefore be repaid by June 1921. It was impossible for Portugal to meet this demand if the loans were decoupled from reparations, given the state of the country's finances. Costa put this sudden demand together with the failure of the Conference of Ambassadors to invite Gustave Ador to act and discerned an anti-Portuguese plot, but Gomes, in London, assured him that there had been no change of attitude towards Portugal. The demand for the repayment of the loan had been born exclusively out of Britain's financial necessity. On 28 May Costa was informed by the secretariat of the Peace Conference that the Conference of Ambassadors, having again deliberated on the issue, had resolved that countries that wanted to avail themselves of Mr Ador's services should address him directly.

On 17 May, Gomes had been warned by the Foreign Office that Portugal's claim to 'special compensation' for acts committed in Africa before 1916 would not be discussed at the forthcoming Spa conference, although the treasury would be pleased to receive a note on the subject so that it might be passed on to the British representatives there. By 20 May, a memoir covering Portuguese demands for compensation had been produced and delivered to the Supreme Council, the Conference of Ambassadors and the new President of the Reparations Commission, Louis Dubois, a former Minister of Commerce and Industry in Clemenceau's cabinet. Costa served his by now well known arguments once again: Portugal had, since the start of the conflict, demonstrated its solidarity with the Allies; it had, just as the war started, and thanks to *an admirable and rightly admired effort*, balanced its finances, which was going to allow it to develop its economy. The war, however, had put a halt to this, since the country had been forced, from the start, to mount military expeditions to secure its colonies and islands. When, after a British request, it had seized German shipping, it had found itself at war with the Central Powers.

Up-to-date figures were now quoted: 34,457 soldiers sent to Africa and 63,062 to France; 3,800 killed in Africa, along with 40,000 wounded, or rendered incapable of work (which included locally recruited men); 1,787 killed in France, along with 12,483 wounded or rendered incapable of work. In all, 273,547 people had lost their lives in the colonies as a result of the conflict; at the conference's going rate of $5,000 each, this amounted to £287,225,000. The cost of fighting the war had also led to an increase in public debt to the order of £233 million. While it had already increased the tax burden on its people, the country was in no position to meet all of its financial obligations on its own: *Portugal, which contributed insofar as its strength allowed to the Allied victory, and which, as a result, emerged victorious from the war, cannot and must not undergo the fate of the defeated when the time comes to negotiate the conditions which the winners will impose on their enemies. Portugal is also entitled to expect that those alongside whom it fought against the common foe, and with whom it has kept itself in strict solidarity, will not permit that it be forgotten and its rights be ignored.*[10]

When all the figures were added up, the Portuguese claim for reparations came, at this stage, to a still provisional 8,641,163,040 gold marks (£432 million), a truly staggering sum. This was not kept secret; in an interview with the *Diário de Notícias*, Afonso Costa went through the memoir in detail. Asked what would happen if Germany was not able to meet its obligations, Costa replied that the country faced bankruptcy, adding, misleadingly, that the highest possible sum that Germany could pay would be distributed to each allied country in accordance with its share of the justified demands for compensation.[11] Describing the Portuguese demands to Sir Eyre Crowe, the Foreign Office's Permanent Under-Secretary, Teixeira Gomes, Portugal's minister in London, remarked, turning logic on its head, that 'one can now begin to understand (because, unfortunately, it is only in figures that we can trust) that the part played by my country in the losses suffered during the war is far from insignificant'.[12]

There was a renewed sense of urgency to Costa's entreaties for information from Lisbon at this, *the decisive moment for the defence of our most important interests*.[13] However, as can be imagined, the British poured cold water on the Portuguese claim. Sir John Bradbury, Britain's representative on the Reparations Commission, wrote that, 'I do not think that figures of the kind set out in the enclosure to your memorandum can serve any useful purpose'. He informed Costa that Portugal was rowing against the tide (evidenced, in any case, by Poincaré's departure from the scene): 'The question which was debated at San Remo and Hythe (a conference held on 15–16 May 1920) was not that of presenting additional claims against Germany in excess of the burden laid upon her by the Treaty but rather of finding a more expeditious method of assessing that burden possibly effecting some reduction in the weight of it, with a view to making possible the restarting of German economic life.'[14]

Costa replied immediately, expressing himself hurt by the content of Bradbury's short missive, since it revealed that no one – not even the British – understood the scale of the losses endured by Portugal during the war. This, he said, might be due to the fact that they occurred in far off Angola and Mozambique, subjected to the ravages of the conflict since 1914. Costa, however, denied that loss of life in the colonies, mostly of civilians, fell outside the scope of the reparations, and that he was making any 'additional' claims in the memoir; he was content to add flesh to the existing Portuguese demand for justice, if required to do so.[15]

The scale of British indignation at the level of Portuguese

damages is, however, testified to by an article which, unexpectedly, and signed by 'a Lisbon correspondent', appeared in *The Times*. This was an unprecedented attack on the Republic and its leading men, which stressed that 'the serious crisis, political, financial, and economic, which afflicts Portugal, if partly the result of the war, is chiefly due to the errors of Republican Governments'.[16] A succession of weak governments had, instead of solving the country's problems, added to them. Army, navy, civil service: all were grossly overstaffed and inefficient, populated by 'parasites who do little but draw their pay'; this was the inevitable result of the move towards liberalism, which had taken Portugal away from its traditional road and into a foreign, imported, system, for which the country was not suited. If the liberal monarchy had been bad, then the Republic was infinitely worse, since it was at the mercy of 'groups of professional revolutionaries, men mostly of no character'. The only way forward for the country was the reconciliation of all men of talent, be they republicans, Catholics, or monarchists. Two figures were singled out for praise in this long and damaging article: *Dom* Miguel, the last absolute monarch, and Sidónio Pais, described as a 'great President'. Costa complained of the article to Xavier Silva, stressing that *The Times* correspondent was *abusing the hospitality granted to him by our country*.[17]

On the day that the article was published, Afonso Costa was still in a good mood. Writing to his daughter, he laid out his future plans. On 4 June, he would sign the peace treaty with Hungary; on the 19th, he would go to Spa and spend a week there. Then he would go on to Brussels, thus completing the greater part of his official functions: *Should Portugal be left in a good position and benefiting from some material compensation I will consider my efforts to have been worthwhile and my official career over. All that will be left to do is sign the Treaty with Turkey (sometime in August), compile the general report on the Delegation's labours and finally write my book about Portugal's participation in the war.* After that, his life would be dedicated to family and friends: *I will turn myself into a Patriarch-Philosopher and tend to my practice, maybe my lecturing, of course my grandchildren and, alongside them, the flowers and fruits of Nature.*[18]

Gomes, meanwhile, was active in London defending Portugal's case, and secured a copy of a letter sent by the Foreign Office's Lancelot Oliphant to Sir John Bradbury, regarding the Portuguese claim. Despite the fact that the Portuguese did not quite understand 'the exact scope of the reparation provisions of the Treaty', Bradbury should still 'exercise his good offices in this matter and assist so far as he properly can the Portuguese delegate by friendly discussion and advice as regards the best method of presenting and pressing their claim'.[19]

The unexpected death of the Portuguese Prime Minister, António Maria Baptista, on 6 June 1920, did not slow down Costa and his team as they geared up for the Spa conference, which, in the meantime, had been postponed. As ever, he kept a watchful eye on domestic developments. Álvaro de Castro seemed set to form a government with Liberal ministers; some time later António José de Almeida cabled Costa, asking him to convince Teixeira Gomes to serve as head of a 'concentration' government, bringing together men of different parties (Gomes refused the invitation, using his health as an excuse).[20]

Costa's requests for information from Lisbon were constant. Had there been a census of Angola's southern regions since the war, so that some evidence might be found for the loss of life alleged by the delegation to have taken place there? Could all legislation covering reparations and war pensions be sent to him? The Spa Conference seemed fixed for 5 July. Writing to his daughter, Costa again stressed the importance of the hour: *Now the most important difficulties for Portugal will be resolved. Now we will find out if, despite the constant errors in our political life, Dr Teixeira Gomes and I still have the prestige and the authority needed for Portugal to be well placed and sufficiently satisfied when it comes to reparations.*[21]

Preparations for Spa continued at a furious pace, with work that should have been carried out over the course of many months being compressed into a few days. On 27 June Costa, Bradbury and their respective staffs met. Costa noted that despite Bradbury's goodwill, the Allies remained reluctant to accept Portuguese estimates of damages. One objection, which was shared by the Belgians, French and British alike, related to compensation for Africans killed during the war, since reparations should only be paid to dependents of the deceased. Costa suddenly developed a sense of racial equality, arguing that what was good for Europeans was good for Africans as well: many families in Angola and Mozambique had been left without their breadwinner, and the Portuguese government had, he claimed, stepped in to make up the shortfall. When Bradbury stated that the compensation for each person killed as a result of the war was too high when applied to 'natives without any trace of civilization', Costa replied that no distinctions were made in the treaty between European dead and others. Bradbury then changed tack, inquiring as to the minimum sum for which Portugal would settle, as a percentage of another country's reparations. Adding a number of caveats, Costa suggested that Portugal could live with £2 for every £25 earned by Great Britain. Since Britain seemed to be asking for £2.5 billion, this would mean £200 million for Portugal, considerably less than the £432 million which he had originally demanded.[22]

The Spa Conference, on which so much rested for Portugal – it would decide, after all, what percentage of reparations each allied country would receive – opened on 5 July. That day, Costa wrote to his daughter, was an anti-climax, as the full German delegation – Costa still referred to them as *boches* – had not yet arrived. Costa remained busy in the days that followed, holding a series of meetings about reparations and discussing the return of Portuguese merchant ships by the Allies with delegates on their way to London to deal with the issue. He also briefed journalists, informing them that while Portugal, in principle, demanded 8 per cent of the total reparations payments, he would be willing, given the reductions being made by other delegations, to accept 2.5 per cent.[23] In the meantime, Costa took the baths in Spa every day, fearing that, since the waters stimulated his appetite, he might be gaining weight.[24] During the negotiations he wrote to his daughter, explaining how intense and difficult his work was; he was unstinting in his praise for the British, who had helped the Portuguese to dodge a blow delivered by the delegates of an undisclosed country which risked *alienating the remaining sympathy of those peoples who esteem it the most*.[25]

By 13 July all seemed well. Lloyd George had risen from his sick-bed to make a supreme effort to bring the parties together in agreement on the larger issues of the conference. Moreover, Sir Eyre Crowe had spoken to Costa, assuring him that Portugal's claim to reparations was now safe. Costa was ecstatic: *Finally, my daughter, it is recognized that Portugal was a useful contributor to the war, and she is given a share*

of the German indemnity, alongside the peoples who fought
– France, England, Italy, Belgium, Serbia, Greece, Romania,
Czechoslovakia and Poland. It should be noted, however, that
the shares of these last five States are yet to be fixed and that
they are proportionately less favourable than ours.[26]

Costa explained that Portugal would receive 0.75 per cent of the total reparations paid by Germany. Comparing losses suffered and reparations received, Portugal was better off than all other countries, with the possible exception of Belgium, he added. In addition to the indemnity, Portugal was allowed to keep all the ships seized in 1916 still afloat and their original cargo and all German property already liquidated in Portugal. Moreover, it still had the arbitration tribunal into pre-1916 events to look forward to. Finally, Costa also expressed the hope that Britain would cancel war debts of £15 million. These early findings were confirmed in another letter written two days later. Although exasperated by ongoing German subterfuges, Costa was by then confident that the Portuguese position would not worsen. All that remained now was for Portugal to take advantage of this diplomatic triumph, through a period of domestic calm and good administration: *Unfortunately, as you say, many of those people know only how to preach and practice insult and foolishness. Fortunately, one day the leading strata, poorly led and burdened by the greatest defects, will be replaced by the working and honest layer of the governed who wish only to be allowed to contribute to the good name of the country. This has always been the case in times of crisis* [...][27]

Two days later, the conference was over. About to return to Paris on the same train as the French delegation, Costa reflected on what had been achieved. As usual, modesty was in short supply: *I can tell you, therefore, that the situation we conquered before* sidonismo, *when I came with Mother to the Inter-Allied Conference of 1917, has been matched and even surpassed. It is a pity that in Portugal governments have not been able or willing to help me, by giving of the country, and of its capacity for work and progress, the excellent impression I was once able to create, with my administration!*[28]

Portugal, Costa claimed, had been left in a privileged position, insofar as it was the only country outside the Great Powers and Belgium to have a guaranteed proportion (the same, in fact, as Japan's) of reparations. Greece, Romania, Yugoslavia and others were handed a pot of 6.5 per cent to divide up among them. Given, however, that Great Britain was awarded 22 per cent of the German reparations, the proportion received by Portugal fell far short of what Costa had announced he was willing to countenance as a minimum. Moreover, Portugal was essentially powerless to affect the final reparations sum, so that in effect it had merely secured an unknown quantity. It was only at the end of April 1921 that the Allies finally settled on the total reparations bill to be paid by Germany, 132 billion gold marks (£6.6 billion). Theoretically, then, just under £50 million should go to Portugal in reparations, but, given the scheme for payment of reparations, Portugal could only look forward to around £1 million per year. Very little money ever materialized; in 1932, the payments dried up completely, after having slowed down considerably in light of the Dawes and Young plans. All of this was, however, in the future. For the moment Costa was determined to call the result a victory and celebrate it.

After Spa, and apart from finding out the final reparations figure, there seemed only one more task to be done, the signing of the peace treaty with Turkey. The Portuguese delegation to the Peace Conference decided, as a result, to call a halt to its mission. Vitorino Guimarães, one of the financial experts attached to the delegation, would continue to deal with the reparations issue; representation at the arbitration tribunal to be named by Gustave Ador could be run from Lisbon, a Portuguese representative – José Maria Vilhena Barbosa Magalhães – having already been named; someone else should be nominated for the Financial Conference to be held shortly in Brussels. *I shall draft my report at no expense to the State as soon as my health allows me to return to work, entrusting in the meantime all the files of this Delegation to Mr Vitorino Guimarães, who might need them. The Portuguese Delegation to the Reparations Commission will be modestly housed in the Hotel Celtic, on the Rue Balzac.*[29]

Despite bringing his involvement in the Peace Conference to a close in August 1920, it was Afonso Costa who represented Portugal at the Brussels Financial Conference in September 1920, after a summer holiday spent with his family. Costa demonstrated how the war had derailed the Republic's – or rather, his – plans for financial stability leading to economic growth. All that had been achieved by 1914 was pulverised by a conflict that Portugal did not want, but could not avoid participating in. And if in the wake of war measures necessary to right the country's books had not yet been taken, it was because the war had sparked off a social crisis that the government had to attend to by meeting the needs of workers. Military expenses continued to mount while the damage suffered in the colonies had also to be addressed.

More striking than this explanation, however, was Costa's attitude towards the German delegation. Before he spoke, a German representative had held the floor, making an appeal for benevolence from the victorious nations so that his country might live. His words were met with loud applause from the delegates of the neutral and Allied nations alike. Costa reacted as if possessed by fury. He mounted the stage, and left his speech to one side. According to the *Diário de Notícias*, 'Mr Afonso Costa turned his back on the Germans until the moment that he accused Germany of having caused the country's deficits and expenses, which so burden its present situation, through its treacherous attacks against the Portuguese in Africa before any declaration of war.'[30]

The fact that the session was being presided over by Gustave Ador might have added to the impression Costa wished to create; it was the Swiss politician who reminded Costa that time was scarce, given the long list of speakers still to be heard. According to this report, 'his intervention had […] corrected the striking effect of the neutrals' applause of the German delegate'.[31] Afonso Costa's mission, in other words, was not yet complete.

8
Between Paris and Lisbon, 1921–1926

In the 1919 elections Afonso Costa had been elected to the Chamber of Deputies by the Democratic Party. Alongside Norton de Matos, he turned down this post, even when the Chamber pleaded with him to reconsider: *What happened to me from 1917 onwards convinced me, unfortunately, that my very presence in a political setting, such as parliament, would serve as a pretext for a renewal of violent struggles among republicans, around my person and against my wishes* […][1]

Costa would be included on the Democratic ticket for Lisbon and elected to every Chamber of Deputies – and there were quite a few – until the Republic's demise in 1926. That year would represent a watershed in his life, with Costa moving from self-imposed exile, resulting from his conscious choice to reside in Paris, to an externally imposed exile, with a formal prohibition from returning to the country he had for so long served. Until 1926, however, there were moments when it seemed as if a return to active politics was imminent.

In the summer of 1920, and in the aftermath of the Spa

Conference, which he was able to present to the country as a triumph – the return of Portugal to the hallowed position he had supposedly brought it to in December 1917 – Afonso Costa was back in the headlines in Portugal for quite other reasons than the Peace Conference. He alerted his countrymen to the growing clerical menace in Portugal. The old campaign against this danger had to be revived, since the Church had been left to its own devices for too long, with no opposition from any quarter. *O Mundo* agreed: 'In the face of this warning, all free-thinkers must unite as a single man, ready to carry out the most intense of actions, guiding themselves by duty and filling the abandoned ranks. The call to muster must be sounded.'[2] Little came of this call, however, and for the time being Costa concentrated on external affairs. He was also invited to fill the position of High Commissioner in Mozambique (which Álvaro de Castro had turned down), eventually refusing on grounds of health.[3]

In November 1920 Afonso Costa represented Portugal at the first meeting of the League of Nations, being elected Vice-President of its Third Commission, the body charged with establishing the International Court of Justice (Léon Bourgeois was its President). During this session of the League's General Assembly, Costa attempted, with some success, to strike at the sanctity of the League's covenant, arguing that while it was included in the Treaty of Versailles, it was separate from it, and could be amended without calling the treaty into question. He did this in order to increase the access of ordinary members to the League's Council – another attempt to roll back an unwelcome part of the Versailles settlement.[4]

With his diplomatic work winding down, there was suddenly a resurgence of interest in the future of Afonso Costa. A series of newspaper articles in January 1921 recounted the events of November and December 1917, explaining that these had represented both a betrayal of Portugal and the Republic and a deliberate attempt to prevent the country from enjoying the benefits of Costa's wartime negotiations in Paris. Serious allegations were made in these articles, including that a U-boat was stationed outside the port of Leixões, ready to sink the ship in which Costa would travel; only an unforeseen change of vessel at the last minute had saved Costa's life from this act of treason by Sidónio Pais and his fellow conspirators. These articles were another step in Costa's postwar rehabilitation, building on the earlier 'triumph' at Spa to suggest that Costa's wartime unpopularity, still widely felt in Portugal, had been misplaced.

In March 1921 Bernardino Machado formed a government, and invited Afonso Costa to return to Lisbon as Finance Minister. Costa politely excused himself, alleging that his return to the cabinet would be an *enormous sacrifice, both moral and physical*, which would in the end prove counterproductive; he affirmed, however, his belief that Machado was uniquely placed to carry out lasting work.[5] His words of appreciation and encouragement were not responded to, by Machado or any other minister, which rankled with Costa: *It seems that the policy adopted in relation to me at the very top is in perfect contrast with the <u>requests for my return</u> addressed to me in O Norte and in letters and telegrams, by some Oporto politicians, people from the provinces and the popular classes.*[6]

Despite this initial setback, the Machado government would make an important contribution to the campaign to rehabilitate Afonso Costa in the eyes of his countrymen. It fell to this cabinet to oversee the high point of the commemoration of Portugal's participation in the war: the burial of two unknown soldiers – one from Africa, one from Flanders – in the medieval monastery of Batalha, built to celebrate victory over Castile at Aljubarrota in 1385 and last resting place of a generation of heroes that included Prince Henry 'the Navigator'. The celebrations that accompanied the return and burial of the two soldiers were timed to coincide with the third anniversary of the CEP's greatest battle. On 9 April 1921, in Lisbon, an enormous parade accompanied the remains of the two soldiers from the parliament building to the Rossio train station; among those who marched were French, Italian and British troops, led by Marshals Joffre and Diaz and General Smith-Dorrien, governor of Gibraltar. Afonso Costa was also present, having arrived in the train that brought Joffre to the Portuguese capital. He lodged at his son-in-law's house in this his first stay in Lisbon since 1917.

On 8 April *O Século* published an interview with Costa, carried out in António José de Almeida's residence. The present moment was, he explained, *sacred*. The people of Portugal, who had understood from the start the need for Portugal's intervention, were now paying their homage to those who had fallen in combat. Asked if this was the hour of vindication for interventionists, Costa unsuccessfully feigned disinterest: *As you can imagine, that means little to me right now. Above all else, the present hour is one of elucidation, an hour full of light which forces miserly spirits to vanish from sight, cowering with fright. It is the radiant hour of truth finally beheld by all.* He continued, *No one will henceforth be allowed to doubt that the people of Portugal, my countrymen, unmatchable in their heroism, went to war fully aware that they were going to defend and safeguard the rights and interests of a* Pátria *that belongs to us all.*[7] Although the reparations question had not yet been completely resolved,

Costa expressed both his confidence that Portugal's rights would be respected and the hope that the Portuguese would always place their common bonds and interests above party politics.

Despite a personal appeal from Costa, which was put up in the Rossio, Lisbon's central square, a crowd still assembled on 8 April to pay its respects to the returned leader. In their hundreds, according to *O Século*, the demonstrators made their way to the home of Fernando de Castro, Costa's son-in-law, hailing Portugal, the Republic and Afonso Costa along the way. Costa greeted the crowd from a window and heard its spokesman make a plea for his return to domestic politics, which he declined, explaining that his foreign mission was not yet over. He added, however, that if needed he would indeed return to work selflessly for the *Pátria* and the Republic, as he was doing abroad.

On 10 April, the day after the military parade,[8] the bodies of the two unknown soldiers were buried at Batalha. One of many speakers at the ceremony, Costa seized the chance to restate the interventionist case. The whole world, as represented by the visiting dignitaries, had come to pay its respects to the Portuguese people; the unknown soldiers, and the present ceremony, justified Portugal's participation in the conflict – and those who had fought to bring it about could now hold their heads up high. Costa then linked the war and his own diplomatic actions during and after the war. The war had been expensive, but it was not, he claimed, the cause of the country's present economic difficulties, which were being felt across the globe. Moreover, the whole world now admired Portugal, and 0.75 per cent of German reparations had been earmarked for Portugal's benefit. Costa finished his address by embracing Machado, 'sealing in that embrace the oath sworn to the country that participation in the war was the most important event in our contemporary history'.[9]

After this promising start, however, 1921 took a turn for the worse. Machado and his Finance Minister, António Maria da Silva asked Costa, on the back of his successes abroad, to secure the holy grail of Portuguese finances – a foreign loan which, guaranteed by the forthcoming reparations payments, might allow for a consolidation of existing debt, the anchoring of the hard-pressed *escudo* and investment in the country's economic development. Costa agreed to carry out this mission. News of the cabinet's intention leaked to the financial world, however, and on 6 May Costa was approached by a financier by the name of Nogueira Pinto on behalf of an Antwerp-based Portuguese firm, the Crédit International de Transit Entrepost et Warrants (usually referred to as the Crédit). Many of the names involved in this enterprise were well known to Costa and respected in Lisbon financial circles. The Crédit promised to open a credit line of $50 million (£12 million) at an interest rate of 7.5 per cent, and commission of 0.25 per cent, to be used exclusively for the purchase of selected products in America – notably coal and wheat. The Crédit claimed to have an understanding with an American financial concern which in turn could act for the American War Finance Corporation, designed, Nogueira Pinto explained, to promote exports in spite of a very strong dollar by providing loans to foreign governments and firms. On 10 May Costa not only advised the government to accept the offer, but actually noted that the Foreign Office in London need not be consulted: there was no time to lose. As no decision was taken in Lisbon, Costa cabled again on 15 May. A conditional acceptance, with some minor points to be negotiated, was sent on 17 May, and a more definitive one on the 21st – the same day on which the government was toppled, in a bizarre episode, by the hitherto loyal, and politically protected, GNR. Nevertheless, negotiations continued, with a representative of the American concern continuing to pile on the pressure. On 28 May the new Liberal Prime Minister, Barros Queiroz, who also acted as Finance Minister, instructed Costa to conclude the negotiations, stipulating that Portugal wanted deliveries, over the course of two years, of 300,000 tons of wheat and 600,000 tons of coal. More than once Barros Queiroz assured Costa of his complete trust when dealing with the minutiae of the negotiations. These continued until late June, when Costa explained the contract had been signed *ad referendum*.

July was a fallow period in relation to this affair, but at the start of August, belatedly, the government asked the advice of its minister in Washington: Who was Mr Jefferson Williams, the face of the American consortium? And what exactly was the War Finance Corporation's role? The minister soon warned the government that it was walking into a trap. Few seemed to know who Williams was, and the War Finance Corporation was designed to lend money to American manufacturers waiting for payment of their products by foreign clients, not to foreign governments. In addition, a similar attempt had recently been made to lure the Italian government into a false loan of $100 million. The generosity of the terms offered to Portugal made it clear that the proposal was not a serious one.

On 24 August *O Mundo* published an article entitled 'The fifty million dollars: The country must know what is happening'. The target of the article was Barros Queiroz, who had stated, in a recent interview, that he 'expected nothing' to come from the Costa-negotiated loan, which had recently become the subject of much speculation. *O Mundo* reacted automatically: since Costa had negotiated it, the loan could not, by definition, be bad for Portugal. Did Barros Queiroz not realize that by leaving such words in the air he was endangering the great man's reputation? Its questions were echoed in the Chamber of Deputies by a Democratic representative, Vasco Borges.[10] Barros Queiroz, while praising Costa – no one could doubt his honesty, intelligence and patriotism – replied that this was not the time to discuss the contract: if the Chamber insisted, he would do so, but he warned the Deputies that they would be performing a poor service to the country. When Borges attacked again, demanding that the Prime Minister explain the situation to the Chamber, Barros Queiroz replied, 'only if I want to'. In so doing, he opened a gap which Borges, and after him much of the press, exploited: parliamentary dignity. As Borges put it, 'the President of the Ministry will submit to Parliament or resign!'[11]

The scandal gathered steam in September. On the 8th, with yet another government in place, Cunha Leal, a rising star in Portuguese politics, addressed the Chamber of Deputies on the loan. He compared the timing of the negotiation of the loan with fluctuations in the exchange rate, making it clear that those in the know had made a killing. Since the credit had been designed to help the government purchase wheat, coal, cotton and iron, there had been less need for the government to purchase sterling on the Lisbon market, which had led to a localized loss in the value of the British currency. Those informed of the deal were able to sell their sterling in time, buying it again when it was at a low, that is, before it became clear that the loan would not go ahead, at which point sterling again shot up in value. Cunha Leal explained that this was why, despite the fact that a contract had been signed between the government and the Crédit, the American consortium had introduced new demands to which the government could not assent.

It fell to a new Finance Minister, Vicente Ferreira, to respond. He did so with the help of original documentation, which was read into the record of the Chamber. The whole series of negotiations became reasonably clear for the first time. Speaker after speaker, beginning with António Maria da Silva, then spoke out against the financiers – either because they had attempted to commit a fraud, or had themselves been defrauded – but took care to spare Afonso Costa. There was one exception – Carvalho da Silva, a monarchist deputy, who asked why it had taken the government until August to begin investigating who precisely Jefferson Williams was. Carvalho da Silva also asked why Costa – an elected deputy, after all – did not come to the Chamber to give his version of events. Rubbing salt in the wound, Carvalho da Silva lamented the fact that despite Portugal's entry into the war, with all the sacrifice that followed, access to credit was still an impossibility.

By 11 September *O Mundo* had made up its mind: the men of the Crédit, 'monarchist conmen', were to blame for what had happened; Afonso Costa had acted as a well-meaning intermediary between the Crédit and the government. The American angle was a pure invention of the conmen; 'Jefferson Williams', if that was his name, was a hired hand, employed to make the con more realistic. None of Costa's actions were in any way suspicious; his honour was 'immaculate'. Later in September Costa finally addressed the issue of the loan in a series of interviews carried out in his mountain residence, Vila Alzira. In these he stressed absolutely that he had refused to deal with anyone other than members of the Crédit, nor did he know where their money came from: they were a reputable firm which had made a business offer and that was good enough for him. However, Costa refuted the thesis that the con had been intended to make a profit from currency exchange. As far as he was concerned, the Crédit's men had agonised over every detail, and had fretted about the difficulties emanating from America, which grew continuously after the contract's signature. One of these had eventually proved impossible to overcome – differing interpretations of the contractual phrase 'inherent expenses', for which the Americans wanted to charge 2 per cent of the total disbursed by the government. It was only at this point that the government began to investigate who Williams was, and that the deal fell apart.

These interviews served only to create more confusion. Most of the republican political establishment had earlier rowed in behind Costa, as we have seen, but its account of events did not square with his. Afonso Costa was tainted with scandal, and would not be able to shake it off; opponents on the left and right would regularly return to it, and it would be mentioned in the same breath as the Furness shipping contract and other 'scandals'. Costa's closing statement on the matter to the *Diário de Notícias* was not one to inspire trust, however: *In the future, governments will have to be more careful. They must deal only with groups capable of answering for their actions.*[12]

In the same interview, Afonso Costa was questioned about his return to domestic politics, and replied that the question was premature. But the desire was undoubtedly there. Once again, though, events in Portugal conspired to keep him at bay. The Barros Queiroz government, although short lived, was remarkable for having organized elections – the one time in the Republic's history that a party other than the PRP was able to do so. The result was a partial victory for the Liberal Party, which was left without an outright majority in the Chamber of Deputies. Another Liberal government, headed by António Granjo, took over, but the PRP simply could not see the merits of being in opposition. Its press conducted ever more savage attacks on Granjo and the Liberals, accusing them of collusion with *sidonistas* and monarchists and of rolling back the Republic's main policies.

On 19 October 1921 elements of the PRP, led by a veteran of the 1891 Oporto rising, Manuel Maria Coelho, leading a traditional brew of civil revolutionaries and enlisted ranks in the navy, stormed to power. This time, though, the coup leaders lost control of their foot-soldiers. The result became known as the '*noite sangrenta*' ('night of blood'). Granjo and a number of political figures who had collaborated with Sidónio Pais, including Machado Santos, were murdered by a group of sailors. Public opinion, at home and abroad, was shocked; the international community made it clear that it would treat Portugal as a pariah until its revolutionary government was deposed. One by one the different factions of the PRP turned their back on the revolutionaries, who eventually resigned. Costa in Paris was appalled by the murder of Granjo (he had less to say on Machado Santos); this time there was no deterministic sociological explanation:

> The 1921 elections resulted in greater diversity in Portugal's parliamentary representation. One newcomer to the Chamber of Deputies, representing the small Catholic Centre Party, was a little-known finance professor from the University of Coimbra, **António de Oliveira Salazar** (1889–1970). He would encourage the view, once in power, that the sight of sterile parliamentary debate had led him to flee Lisbon after a single session, but there is little proof of this; he was elected to a number of parliamentary commissions, and would run again, unsuccessfully, for parliament. His early parliamentary career was only cut short by the events of 19 October 1921.

Granjo was a great figure of the Republic […] *We suffer for our country, we are ashamed of what goes on there. Only an exemplary punishment could assuage the terrible impression caused abroad by these events and the discredit which they heaped upon us.*[13]

Quite apart from its impact on Portuguese politics – chaos followed eventually by a period of stabilization under Democratic rule – the *noite sangrenta* forced Afonso Costa to rearrange his plans for the immediate future. He explained to his daughter that he had hoped to return definitively to Portugal within a year, but that for the moment he and Alzira were forced to remain in France – for how long, it was still impossible to tell.[14] Since he was free to return to Portugal, and there were no informal requests, as in late 1918, for him to remain abroad, it is clear that Costa feared for his safety; he nevertheless cabled António José de Almeida, who had been deeply shaken by events, asking him to stay on as President, *for the salvation of the Pátria and the Republic.* Costa's pessimism was great, and he included the *noite sangrenta* in a cycle of catastrophes that had begun in December 1917: *Looking back on events in these four years of perdition and criminal madness, we cannot but be amazed by one thing: that the* Pátria *is still alive.*[15]

In January 1922 elections gave the Democrats a clear majority in Congress, but Costa refused António José de Almeida's invitation to head a government. Almeida served out his bitter term as President of the Republic, being replaced in the summer of 1923 by Teixeira Gomes, whose candidacy Afonso Costa had backed. It was Gomes' intention to invite Costa, as soon as possible, to form a cabinet. This became possible in October of that year, when a period of relative stability came to an end. When Gomes began to sound out party leaders as to whom the next head of government should be, he was assured that the PRP would support a Costa cabinet, as would, in fact, most other political groupings. Costa was then consulted privately – through Germano Martins – about the job. He immediately let it be known that he would accept. The long exile seemed over. According to O *Século*, public opinion thought Costa to be the most suitable candidate for the position, and his supporters headed for the various train stations the *Sud-Express* would stop at, to greet their returning idol. One immediate consequence of Costa's return was a fall in the value of sterling in Lisbon.

Costa arrived in Lisbon on the morning of 6 November. En route he had spoken to the press. The country's international position was secure, as was its standing with the Reparations Commission, and, while not going into detail about his plans, Costa outlined what was required from the people of Portugal: there had to be trust, patience and the collaboration of all in order to move the country forward. The Rossio station, where Sidónio Pais had been murdered some five years previously, was full of well-wishers; but the ever cautious Costa alighted on the outskirts of the city and made his way home by car. The next day he initiated contact with the various political figures: Teixeira Gomes, António Maria da Silva, Norton de Matos and Álvaro de Castro (now leader of the Nationalist Party, the main opposition, born out of the fusion of the Liberals and Castro's own Democratic dissenters, the *Reconstituintes*). His intentions were announced: he was only willing to lead a 'national' government, capable of carrying out a 'national' policy. The press, notably O *Século*, applauded this stance, saying it fitted in with the wishes of the population: administration, rather than politics, was the order of the day, and the political parties must give him what he wanted in order to govern.

After dinner with Gomes, Costa stepped into hostile territory: the offices of the newspaper *A Luta*, where Sidónio Pais had plotted his overthrow. Awaiting him were members of the Nationalist Party's Directorate, who heard Costa make a plea for their help. He asked for a lot: a free hand in the naming of ministers from all parties *before* elaboration of a programme of government, and subsequent parliamentary support for the 'national' government. The two-hour meeting did not go well, with a number of Nationalists objecting to the possible immolation, in case of failure, of all republican parties, including their own, whose support might more profitably be held back in reserve. While promising their party's support for a Costa-led Democratic government, the Directorate decided to consult its parliamentary representatives before giving a definitive answer to Costa. This meeting took place immediately after Costa's withdrawal from *A Luta*'s offices, and took little over an hour. Opinion, led by Ginestal Machado, president of the Directorate, was overwhelmingly against allowing Costa to cherry-pick party members for his government; only Álvaro de Castro, Costa's choice for the Ministry of the Colonies, urged his party colleagues to consider the issues fully. The matter was entrusted to another party body, its Consultative Junta, made up of the Directorate, parliamentary party old and new, ex-ministers and ex-civil and colonial governors.

On 9 November the Lisbon press announced that Afonso Costa's attempt to form a national government had come to an end. The Nationalists had decisively – almost unanimously, according to newspaper reports – rejected Costa's condition of being able to choose party members as ministers. Once again Castro was one of the few moderate voices; according to O *Século*, in his words and those of another speaker,

Hélder Ribeiro, 'great esteem and affection' for Costa could be found.[16] One of their most vehement opponents was Cunha Leal. At the end of the Nationalists' meeting a motion was passed which restated the party's belief in its yet untested ability to govern the country and its refusal to participate in a government for which no programme had been given. The failure of such a cabinet 'would deprive the Republic of a party free of responsibility for the past'.[17]

After the meeting Ginestal Machado informed Costa of the motion and Costa, having briefed Gomes of the situation, announced that his efforts had come to naught. Some bitterness was evident in his interview with O *Século*, published on 10 November. Questioned about Nationalist reservations about his programme, Costa replied: […] *what reservations could there be, at this moment when we have a deficit greater than 300,000* contos *(£2.5 million), about the financial ability of the man who, in 1913, launched the country's financial regeneration, achieving, as attested to later by the figures, the balancing of the budget? Must I subject myself to an exam before being allowed to govern? Were not my past and my distance from party life sufficient to dispel all reservations? I would have thought so, all the more so since from afar, on account of circumstances known by all, I continued to love my country, and love it more every day.*[18]

This was not the last time that Costa was spoken of as a potential prime minister, but it was certainly the closest he ever came to returning to national politics. In June 1924 the idea of a Costa-led national government was again floated. Álvaro de Castro, Prime Minister since December 1923, embarked on a programme of financial reform, and in late February informed Costa that it was his intention to give way to him as head of government in June, once controversial legislation had been ratified.[19] Although there was intense press speculation in June that this transfer of power might actually occur, it never went ahead, Costa finding again that it was impossible to create a cabinet to his liking. An appeal from the PRP Congress in June 1925 to return to Portugal and head a partisan government was ignored. *O Libertador*, a radical newspaper with little to offer but bile, pictured Costa receiving the party's telegram while escorting his mistress – 'a distinguished actress, a woman with dark blond hair, tall, slim, elegant, wearing small bronzed shoes and a silk dress, half-naked' – down a Paris boulevard. Reading the telegram, Costa crumples it and throws it away, explaining merely that 'it's my caretakers, begging for my return to Portugal'.[20]

This, then, was the image that his enemies would paint, time and time again, in the future: a plutocrat whose wealth was derived from lucrative contracts with state-owned enterprises, for whom he acted as an attorney, and who was too comfortable in his Parisian exile to return home. He did, however, continue to represent Portugal at international events. In 1925 he attempted to negotiate, unsuccessfully, a resolution to the country's war debt in London, and led the Portuguese delegation to the League of Nations, being elected president of its Fourth Commission (Secretariat and Finances). He was in Geneva again in March of the following year for a special session of the League, during which he was elected President of the General Assembly. The honour bestowed on him was great, and Costa relished the attention, writing, *I hope that this homage to Portugal and to me gives satisfaction to good patriots and to my friends. The others – those who tried to ruin me in 1917 – must at this hour be annoyed with this noisy demonstration – in the name of 36 nations of the world – that <u>I am not yet finished</u>. It would* *be such an easy thing to increase now our prestige and the consideration of others for us! However, it would require this very elementary thing: WISDOM!* However, Costa's role was slight since the main business of the special session – the admission of Germany – was largely conducted in the Executive Council.

After a week's negotiations, the Council informed the Assembly that it had failed to find consensus on the inclusion of Germany as a permanent member of the Council. As a result, Germany would not be requesting membership of the League. Since the Assembly had barely met, Costa's duties were protocol in nature. They included a banquet for 100 people followed by a reception for 300: *the most notable statesmen of the whole World and some of their ladies will come to dinner or to the reception*, Costa explained proudly.[21] In a closing speech, Costa reaffirmed his faith in the League and expressed the hope that the business at hand would be resolved at its next session. The military coup of May 1926 would mean that Costa did not lead the Portuguese delegation again, and soon ensured that his exile became a permanent one.

9
Exile, Death and Legacy

On 28 May 1926, General Gomes da Costa, formerly commanding officer of the CEP's 2nd Division, initiated what he termed a 'march on Lisbon' to clear away the Democratic political establishment, still led by two great survivors of Portuguese politics, Bernardino Machado (in his second mandate as President of the Republic) and António Maria da Silva. The successful coup did not give way to a clear political situation, since the army, now in charge of the country's destiny, was too deeply divided to follow a coherent line. Years of confusion would follow with all of the contending factions agreeing on one thing only: that the PRP must not be allowed to return to power. Costa was not an immediate target for the revolutionaries, and in November 1926 he made a brief return to Portugal, not realizing that it would be his last.

Costa's residence abroad, for the rest of his life, would be the discreet yet comfortable Hotel Vernet, Paris; his offices were located in the Rue du Faubourg de Saint Honoré. Much of his time was spent alone, since his family was still domiciled in Portugal. Holidays in Spain or the south of France brought them together. Morale rose and fell with the changing circumstances, although he tried to keep a brave face in his personal correspondence, increasingly subjected to postal censorship. In the 1930s, Shirley Temple films served as a substitute for seeing his granddaughter.[22]

As the dictatorship's hold over the country deepened, and initial armed revolts against it failed, Costa awoke to the dangers posed by those who wanted to create a lasting authoritarian, or even fascist, solution. He participated in the foundation of a 'League for the Defence of the Republic', in Paris, and accepted the role of Minister of Finance in a government to be led by Álvaro de Castro, with whom he became, politically, especially close. It was the League's wish that a new form of republic might be created, one which prioritized social improvements and in which the parties of old no longer operated. This led the PRP's leadership to ignore the League's workings, trusting as it did its own ability to reverse the dictatorship and take up where it had left off in May 1926. The League produced pamphlets and newspapers to be spirited into Portugal, and organized its own conspiracies, but to no avail. Another field of action was the League of Nations, with which the Portuguese government was trying to negotiate a loan: Costa and others warned foreign leaders that a restored Republic would not feel obliged to repay loans contracted by an illegal government.

Costa and his fellow conspirators were involved in a high profile revolutionary attempt in the spring of 1931, which saw republican forces take control of the island of Madeira, and which had offshoots in the Azores and some African colonies. Coinciding as this did with the beginning of the Second Republic in Spain, these revolts created real tension in Lisbon, from which military expeditions were sent to subdue – with eventual success – the rebellious territories. From Madrid, Costa warned his family to leave Lisbon for the coast, since he expected *severe* events in Lisbon as a result of the *great Movement* that would restore the Republic.[23]

Despite the setback, hopes were pinned by Costa and others on cooperation of the republican regime in Spain (Costa having met with leading figures of the Second Republic, such as Indalecio Prieto), which allowed conspiratorial bases to be set up near the Portuguese border and the stockpiling of weapons. The year 1932 saw a political amnesty decreed by the Lisbon government, now led by António de Oliveira Salazar. Costa was one of only four civilians mentioned in the list of fifty exceptions, which also included his eldest son, Sebastião, and Bernardino Machado.[24] That same year the 'Paris League', as it was generally known, dissolved itself; Costa hoped to create a 'Supreme Committee' capable of coordinating all opposition – republicans, Socialists, Communists, trade unionists, intellectuals and Masons – to Salazar.

Little progress was made in the years that followed, despite the heightening of tension between Costa and Salazar. At the slightest action by Costa, Salazar's New State would put its propaganda machine, starting with its daily newspaper, the *Diário da Manhã*, in motion against the exiled politician, repeating well worn accusations of naked ambition and greed (as evidenced by lucrative contracts with large Portuguese concerns such as the Banco Nacional Ultramarino and the Companhia dos Diamantes), open corruption (the Furness deal, the $50 million loan) and cowardice (the attack on Sampaio Bruno, the cab ride on the night of 3 October 1910, the attempt to avoid capture in 1917 by hiding in a kitchen lift), and so on.

When, in November 1932, the *Diário de Notícias* published an interview with Costa in which he affirmed his broad sympathy with socialism, the *Diário da Manhã* had a field day. Seizing on Costa's description of his exercise routines and diet (the health-conscious Costa had stopped having dinner, on his doctor's advice), the New State's mouthpiece compared him to Gandhi, in a sustained pun based on the verb *comer*, which means both to eat and to enrich one's self. Having gorged himself for years, Costa now was forced to 'eat' less: 'Could we, the conquerors and lords of India, afford to cause a bad impression, in the eyes of that same India, by not possessing a Gandhi? The real one, when he feels like it, sulks and refuses to eat. Ours, for the moment, has only stopped having dinner. But should the *Pátria* demand it, he can go further still!'[25]

In February 1934 the *Diário da Manhã* published an interview with the driver who had transported Afonso Costa on the night of 3/4 October 1910, as the triumphant republican revolt was beginning. Alfredo Gomes explained that the story published by *O Mundo* in 1911 was false, since it had twisted his account in order to make Costa look braver. Moreover, according to Gomes, *O Mundo*'s journalists had refused to believe that, in his panic, Costa had exclaimed 'Oh, my God, they are going to kill me here'; they simply could not countenance that he might have appealed to a divine power in his time of need.

The year 1934 saw renewed interest in Costa's activities, due to a scandal which broke in Spain regarding the links, in 1931, between its government and Portuguese opposition forces, links which had as their lynchpin and financial backer Basque shipbuilder Horacio Echevarrieta Mauri. The scandal rumbled on for months and culminated in a special sitting of the National Assembly, as Portugal's parliament was now styled, organised to denounce the treason of the exiled opposition. One of Salazar's oldest friends and closest collaborators, Mário de Figueiredo, chronicled the links between republicans on both sides of the border. Working from official intelligence documents cited by an investigating Spanish magistrate, Figueiredo highlighted Afonso Costa's role in a plot to smuggle weapons into Portugal. The asides heard in the Chamber were telling:

> 'Always him …'
> 'Where there is treason there you will find him.'
> 'He is always the instigator of bad deeds by the Portuguese!'
> 'A traitor to the *Pátria*!' [26]

In Figueiredo's explanation of events, Echevarrieta was hoping that a new Portuguese government, installed with his help, would proceed to re-equip the country's fleet with ships built by his company. Prime Minister Manuel Azaña, for his part, had given his blessing to the enterprise.

Afonso Costa's final opportunity to participate in the overthrow of Salazar's New State came with the Spanish Civil War of 1936: given Salazar's open support for Franco's rebels, a republican triumph might well lead to the overthrow of the New State. It was in the context of the war in Spain that a Portuguese 'Popular Front' was created, again in the hope of attracting the support of all opposition forces.

One tragic consequence of the Spanish conflict, however, was the near impossibility of Costa seeing his extended family: the distance from Portugal, and the longing to return home, grew accordingly: *As much as I want to avoid writing about Spain in my letters, I cannot but remember the house we rented, just one year ago, on the adorable beach of Ondarreta … near to where a terrible struggle is at this moment being waged. No! I cannot hope to go this year, even if late in the season, to such places. You* [his daughter, Maria Emília] *go, with the children, to a Portuguese beach, with your Mother, and count on me: I never forget you and I never renege on my promises.*[27]

That month, September, he celebrated his 44th wedding anniversary alone, and claimed to be looking forward to his 50th – and even his 75th. He had entered his sixties, he wrote, in fine health, something he was sure filled his enemies with fury. But on 11 May 1937 Afonso Costa died from a sudden bout of angina pectoris.

Costa left no lasting legacy behind him. The post-war Republic was a different regime to the one he had helped to build from 1910 to 1914. Like all 'advanced' parliamentary democracies, its radical edge had been blunted by Bolshevik revolution, and the Democratic Party stopped presenting itself as a vanguard of the people, becoming instead the defender of bourgeois values. In truth, only his anti-clerical stance had given Costa his revolutionary credentials and a dangerous veneer; now, even that had become meaningless. Under Sidónio Pais the law of separation was toned down and diplomatic ties with the Holy See re-established, and this did not change after 1919. Catholic political opinion was concentrated in one party, the Catholic Centre, which affirmed time and again its willingness to cooperate with the Republic, and even to furnish it with ministers. Unwilling to follow a more radical policy, and torn into many and bitterly opposed factions whose infighting prevented them from administering the country well, the Republic's political leaders saw the distance that separated them from the people of their country grow. After the war there had been no extension of the suffrage, almost no constitutional reform and very little in the way of social concessions to the poorer classes that might reconcile them to the regime. There was little scope for renewal; social mobility was limited, and the country's educated youth was moving steadily to the beat of new, right-wing, drums, with different forms of nationalism and authoritarianism vying for dominance. By the Republic's last years, little was expected of Afonso Costa, his services in Paris nearly forgotten.

What had been neither forgotten nor forgiven was Costa's role in Portugal's intervention in the First World War. As the *Diário da Manhã* put it in 1935, during one of its regular anti-Costa campaigns, '[The generation] that went to war will never be able to forget, if not the fact of our intervention, then certainly the inhuman cruelty with which they were thrown into the furnace of Africa, and the foreign lands of France, bereft of all they needed, in material and moral terms.'[28]

This intervention, which Costa had hoped might strengthen the regime, wounded it fatally. Afonso Costa's failure to deliver on his promise of a book with the definitive account of Portugal's intervention in the war contributed to this process. Not even the news in 1936 that Brito Camacho's wartime writings were being republished posthumously stirred him to act, despite promises to the contrary.[29]

The Treaty of Versailles, of course, meant little for Portugal. Costa's ephemeral triumph when it came to reparations eventually came to naught, given Germany's success in bringing the payments to an early end. Arrangements for arbitration of Portugal's claims against Germany for pre-1916 actions in Africa yielded even less; they proved to be an elaborate and overly long waste of time and energy. In January 1921, the Portuguese and German delegations (the first led by Barbosa de Magalhães) had met for the first time, but a judgement was only handed out in July 1928 – well after the fall of the First Republic.[30] The amassing of information and the hearing of witnesses had taken years; each incident in Africa, notably events in Naulila, was teased out in great detail. Aloïs de Meuron, the arbitrator named in 1920, eventually determined that Germany should repair the damages provoked by its acts of aggression, including Naulila; the total reparation sum was not then announced. Hopes were high in this respect for Portugal, since the Swiss arbitrator had deemed that the German authorities were responsible for all the damage provoked during and in the wake of the Battle of Naulila. On 30 June 1930 the reparations payments were finally determined: 48,226,468.30 gold marks, of which 45 million was recompense for events in Africa.[31]

This was not, however, the end of the affair. By the time the bill was arrived at, the German government had already begun to tie whatever agreement for compensation payments emerged from Lausanne to the recently agreed Young Plan, which scaled down German reparations. Portugal, as would be expected, attempted to block this linkage. No compromise was possible between the two countries, but Portugal had to ratify the Young Plan in order to remain eligible for the other, standard, reparations payments. Publication of de Meuron's judgement did not alter this stance, and it was only in July 1931 that the impasse was broken: Portugal would sign up to the Young Plan while a new round of arbitration would determine the fate of the Lausanne payments in the light of the new circumstances. This tribunal met in due course, and submissions were heard in February 1933; on the 16th sentence was passed, stating that Germany was not obliged to make any payments outside those stipulated in the Young Plan. Portugal had been well and truly defeated.

Afonso Costa had hoped that the treaty, and especially the subsequent negotiations, might rehabilitate interventionists and their brand of republic, but this never came to pass. Worse still, for his reputation, was the advent of Salazar. Costa never came to grips with the nature of the New State. At first he viewed it as a military dictatorship, which could be reversed by a military counter-coup: but it was the army's hatred of the Democratic Party that allowed officers of very different political outlooks to work together, accepting a civilian leader. Then, paralyzed by Salazar's Catholic background, Costa saw the emerging regime as a final burst of Jesuitical reaction, a last attempt by his old enemies to reassert their authority over Portugal. But Salazar was much more than this. Born into humbler circumstances than Costa, in a similar part of the country, Salazar married a comparable work ethic with a steady religious faith and a detestation of parliamentary regimes. While Costa was dogmatic, believing that there was a perfect political and social model, and that Portugal should be altered in order to fit that mould, Salazar was highly pragmatic, allowing his regime to change slowly with the times (provided he remained in control) but seeking, as he put it often in his speeches, to reconcile the nation with the State.

In an interview with the *Diário de Notícias*, in October 1933, Salazar announced that henceforth his government would go on the offensive against the opposition: 'I cannot accept the small-mindedness and the ridiculous nature of the petty worries of certain groups, and sub-groups, in the face of national realities! I do not understand and cannot tolerate that half a dozen good-for-nothings should spend their life plotting my destiny and that of my collaborators, while the men in the seats of Power struggle against the great national problems, and solve them!'[32]

The most important of these 'good-for-nothings' was

Afonso Costa, who remained the opposition's trump card, the 'other' Finance Minister, beside Salazar, capable of righting the budget. An interview Costa gave to a Brazilian journalist, José Jobim, was published in 1934, in Rio de Janeiro, as a small pamphlet, *A Verdade Sobre Salazar* (The Truth about Salazar). In it, Costa accused Salazar of fiddling the books in order to produce illusory budget surpluses, and of establishing a clerical regime in Portugal. In reply, Salazar penned an official note answering the allegations, and focusing on the subject of education. Men like himself had been educated in an increasingly positivist spirit, which relied on the observation of the real world: his teachers had relied on 'texts, tables, objects, maps, statistics and experiments'. Previous generations, however – men like Afonso Costa – were chained to the world of theory, and doomed to argue themselves to exhaustion in the face of the living proof which undermined their points. Their arguments were sterile, but arguing was all they knew. That Salazar had been educated in a seminary, as everyone knew, added piquancy to the argument. Costa and Jobim produced a reply to the official note,[33] in which Costa described, and magnified, his role in the denial of a foreign loan to the Portuguese dictatorship. Salazar did not bite again; he had no wish to be dragged into a polemical argument with Costa. Others could do the job for him. One writer, Alberto Guimarães, weighed in with his *A Verdade Sobre Afonso Costa* in 1935, dredging up, once again, the by now familiar stories: of political rivals compromised, clients fleeced and the public purse abused. The chapter on the war, for example, dealt exclusively with the Furness contract: Costa would always be remembered, Guimarães assured his readers, as a war profiteer, someone who speculated on the misery of others.

Salazar's New State, moreover, presented itself as the anti-Republic. For decades to come the regime would be sold to the people as a modern antithesis to the chaotic scenes that had preceded it, in an endless succession of governments, coups, and pointless elections. In the increasingly nationalist 1930s and beyond, this was an argument which made sense in Portugal; few mourned the passing of the old order. Salazar kept Portugal out of the Second World War, for which most in Portugal were thankful. The New State began to run into difficulty only when a generation which could no longer remember the First Republic became politically conscious and unhappy with Salazar's increasingly arbitrary and reactionary rule. Salazar's decision to praise Afonso Costa in a 1966 speech commemorating the 40th anniversary of the 'National Revolution', as one of the 'great names' who had preceded him as Finance Minister,[34] revealed just how generalised ignorance of the First Republic and its leading figure had become four decades after its demise.

The New State outlived its founder and limped on until 1974; in the end, reform was practically impossible, because it would interfere with the defence of Portugal's colonial empire. It was the army, tired of fighting three increasingly pointless wars in Africa, which overthrew Marcelo Caetano's government in the 'carnation revolution' of April 1974, and paved the way for something new, as yet undecided. In the year and a half that followed, as the army's different factions struggled for political control of the country, in conjunction with long-standing or brand-new political parties of all hues, different political futures were discussed for Portugal. Although the choice of the majority of Portuguese was eventually respected, and a parliamentary democracy established, there was almost no sense that a bridge was being built to the First Republic, a regime about which few really knew anything.

Some historians attempted to present the Republic as a worthy predecessor, and Afonso Costa as a father of Portuguese democracy; of these, AH de Oliveira Marques was the most important. It was, however, a vain attempt, which never caught on with other historians or the general public. And although the highly successful Socialist Party, led by Mário Soares, carried in its genetic blueprint, among other currents, the republican inheritance, the post-1974 parliamentary system was built in such a way as to avoid the possibilities of a return to the pre-1926 scenario, introducing universal suffrage, a popularly elected president capable of dissolving parliament, large electoral circles designed to make *caciquismo* an impossibility in national politics, and a good working relationship with the Catholic Church. This was a new departure, not a return to Afonso Costa's Portugal.

Notes

Preface

1. Arquivo Histórico Militar (AHM), Lisbon, 1st Division, 36th Section, Box 36; letter, Paris, 26 March 1920, Afonso Costa to the Minister of Foreign Affairs. In the letter, Afonso Costa did not translate the verbal exchange from its original French. Clemenceau's words were 'voilá l'homme que rien ne peut retenir!', to which Costa replied 'oui, parce qu'il a raison!'.

1 A Republic is Born

1. Pedro Lains, *Os Progressos do Atraso: Uma Nova História Económica de Portugal* (Imprensa de Ciências Sociais, Lisbon: 2003). All translations in the book are my own.

2. Joel Serrão and A H de Oliveira Marques (eds), *Nova História de Portugal*, Vol XI *Portugal da Monarquia para a República* (Presença, Lisbon: 1991) p 413.

3. This was in response to the 'Calmon scandal', in which the Brazilian consul in Oporto, José Calmon, accused clerical elements of attempting to abduct his daughter and deliver her to a convent against his will.

4. This was not the last word on the issue; in 1899 Portugal and Great Britain signed the Treaty of Windsor, by which Great Britain agreed to guarantee the territorial integrity of Portugal and its empire.

5. Afonso da Costa, 'A Federação Académica', in *O Ultimatum* (Coimbra), 23 March 1890. Reprinted in A H de Oliveira Marques (ed), *Afonso Costa* (Arcádia, Lisbon: 1972) p 247, hereafter Marques (ed)*Afonso Costa*.

6. Marques (ed), *Afonso Costa*, p 253.

7. One early biographer described his rapid ascent from undergraduate to lecturer as 'absolutely unique'. José Agostinho, *Dr. Affonso Costa* (Typographia Bayard, Lisbon: 1907) p 10, hereafter Agostinho, *Dr Affonso Costa*.

8. Ismael da Silva, *O Dr. Afonso Costa e a sua obra (1897–1915)* (M Pinto Vieira, Lisbon: 1915) pp 7–8.

9. He who laughs last laughs longest. João Chagas, *O Norte* (Oporto), 22 June 1900. Quoted in Marques (ed), *Afonso Costa*, p 108.

10. Afonso Costa's wealth would provide endless ammunition for his critics, and would be dragged up time and time again as evidence of his cupidity and corruption.

11. João Medina calls attention to the lack of modesty, or sense of proportion, of Afonso Costa's Masonic name, 'Plato'. João Medina, 'Quatro retratos de vultos políticos da I República: Machado Santos, Afonso Costa, João Chagas e Sidónio Pais', *Clio*, 2 (1997), pp 159–60.

12. *Diário da Câmara dos Deputados* (Lisbon), 20 November 1906.

13. Agostinho, *Dr. Affonso Costa*, p 4.

14. Marques (ed), *Afonso Costa*, p 111.

15. Such a strategy did not come easily to Afonso Costa, who in his prison diary reflected on the threat posed by bomb-makers: 'It does not seem to me as if the problem posed by *bombs* will have an easy solution. Those madmen who one day began to manufacture them have gathered proselytes and imitators, who were not troubled by the arrest of some and the death of others. Such a terrible problem will be solved only by good government or extensive education'. Marques (ed), *Afonso Costa*, p 112.

2 Taking Charge, 1910–1914

1. *O Mundo* (Lisbon), 21 November 1910.

2. João Chagas would later write that Afonso Costa had taken steps to secure a passage aboard a ship in the Tagus when it looked like the fighting had taken a turn for the worst. João Chagas, *Diário*, Vol 3, *1918* (Edições Rolim, Lisbon: 1987) p 108, hereafter João Chagas, *Diário*.

3. *O Mundo* (Lisbon), 11 October 1910. This report also covers other interviews carried out by Afonso Costa that dawn. The Cardinal Patriarch's secretary was described as 'lamentably effeminate'. Another interviewee, a Jesuit, told Costa that 'to bring back Pombal's laws, old and seditious, is absurd'. According to *O Mundo*, 'the Minister of Justice replied with decisive arguments and the man became demonstrably agitated, declaring, in the end, that he will leave as soon as possible for Spain […]'.

4. *O Mundo* (Lisbon), 14 October 1910.

5. See, in this regard, Rui Ramos, 'Depoimento – O sentido histórico da I República Portuguesa', in António Reis (ed), *A República Ontem e Hoje* (Edições Colibri: Lisbon, 2002) p 49.

6. *O Mundo* (Lisbon), 9 January 1911.

7. *O Mundo* (Lisbon), 16 January 1911.

8. At this time António José de Almeida informed *The Times*' correspondent in Lisbon that 'the members of the Provisional Government are resolved to work harmoniously together to defend their work as one responsible body'; after that, and the resulting approbation or condemnation, 'each group [would] go its own way'. Nevertheless, the same correspondent wrote that the rift between Almeida's 'Conservative Republicans' and Costa's 'Radicals' was becoming 'daily wider'. *The Times* (London), 9 March 1911.

9. There has been considerable debate about whether or not this forecast was made, but Costa himself referred to the forecast as a fact in a speech made on 17 September 1911, at Lisbon's Geographical Society, during a ceremony in which he was awarded a silver ink-well. For the text of the speech, see *O Mundo* (Lisbon), 18 September 1911.

10. Carlos de Oliveira, *Lei da Separação do Estado das Igrejas Anotada por Carlos de Oliveira. Com um Prefácio do Dr Affonso Costa* (Companhia Portuguesa Editora, Oporto: 1914), Preface.

11. Richard A H Robinson, 'Os Católicos e a Primeira República', in Nuno Severiano Teixeira and António Costa Pinto (eds), *A Primeira República Portuguesa: Entre o Liberalismo e o Autoritarismo* (Edições Colibri, Lisbon: 2000) pp 97–8.

12. *O Mundo* (Lisbon), 21 April 1911. The same newspaper claimed that thousands of congratulatory telegrams descended on the government as a result of the law, many being sent by priests.

13. The Chamber of Deputies was elected for three years, while each Senator sat for six years, half of the Chamber being elected every three years. One could vote for the Chamber at the age of 25, and for the Senate at the age of 35.

14. *O Mundo* (Lisbon), 25 October 1911.

15. Interview of Afonso Costa with *A Capital* (Lisbon), 27 September 1911, reprinted in *O Mundo* (Lisbon) the following day.

16. Afonso Costa's words of greeting in the Chamber of Deputies were decidedly cold. He lamented that members of the Provisional Government were not allowed to continue in its task, which would have been the *sole constitutional, popular, and truly Portuguese solution.* Neither Chagas nor four of his other ministers were members of parliament, which Costa declared an oddity in a representative regime; and, while welcoming Chagas's description of his cabinet as 'anti-clerical', Costa objected to the stated aim of 'pacification' of the 'republican family': struggles between republicans would be loyal and remain within the realm of ideas, wherein a vigorous debate was to be welcomed. *O Mundo* (Lisbon), 5 September 1911.

17. *O Mundo* (Lisbon), 30 October 1911.

18. *O Mundo* (Lisbon), 18 September 1911.

19. Marques (ed), *Afonso Costa*, p 338.

20. Marques (ed), *Afonso Costa*, p 336.

21. The original Constituent Assembly had been split into a Senate and a Chamber of Deputies in a move of doubtful legality. See João B Serra, 'O Sistema Político da Primeira República', Teixeira and Pinto (eds), *A Primeira República Portuguesa*, p 113.

22. According to Rui Ramos, 'the percentage of citizens with electoral power returned to 1860 levels – a regression of some 50 years'. Rui Ramos, 'Depoimento – O sentido histórico da I República Portuguesa', in Reis (ed), *A República Ontem e Hoje*, p 49.

3 Portugal at War, 1914–1917

1. Augusto Soares believed that the presidency of the Republic was the source of leaks regarding diplomatic information; he was told by one Portuguese diplomat that 'sending the notes to Belém [the Presidential palace] was the same as informing Guimarães at *A Capital*'. A H de Oliveira Marques (ed), *O Segundo Governo de Afonso Costa 1915–1916* (Europa-América, Lisbon: 1974) p 39.

2. Over a year later, Afonso Costa informed his government that during this period he had been approached in Lisbon by a Belgian, Baron Leowen (*sic*), charged by the Allied governments with asking him for help in securing the 40 artillery pieces, more important, at that moment, than a full division. Costa claimed to have told him *were I to be in government, I would not give you a single piece without Portuguese soldiers.* Marques (ed), *O Segundo Governo de Afonso Costa*, p 37, hereafter Marques (ed), *O Segundo Governo.*

3. There is evidence to suggest that Bernardino Machado was initially ambivalent about intervening in the war,

but that he changed his mind once Afonso Costa made intervention part of his 'republican mininum', a policy which no good republican could oppose.

4. Marques (ed), *Afonso Costa*, p 377.

5. The *Morning Post* (London), under the headline 'Portuguese Revolt – The Rabble's Victory – A Gloomy Outlook', claimed that 'one will frankly have to consider it [Portugal] in the category of Chile, or Morocco, or Mexico'. António Cabral (ed), *Cartas d'el Rei D. Manuel II* (Livraria Popular de Francisco Franco, Lisbon : 1933), p 202.

6. This was a cabinet in which civilians barely outnumbered military men: officers had control of the War, Navy, Colonies, and Public Instruction portfolios. It also saw a balance struck between the different factions of the Democratic Party, including as it did the ex-*carbonário* António Maria da Silva at *Fomento* and ex-monarchists such as João Catanho de Meneses (Justice) and Captain Alfredo Rodrigues Gaspar (Colonies). Norton de Matos was also an ex-monarchist.

7. Marques (ed), *O Segundo Governo*, p 10.

8. AHM, Lisbon, 1st Division, 35th Section, Box 1298, Confidential Report, 9 October 1916, director of postal censorship to the director general of the Ministério dos Negócios Estrangeiros (MNE).

9. Marques (ed), *O Terceiro Governo de Afonso Costa 1917* (Livros Horizonte, Lisbon: 1977) p 60.

10. Quoted in *ibid*, p 22.

11. *O de Aveiro* (Aveiro), 6 May 1917.

12. According to the British Legation, 'it was rumoured that at least 200 people had been killed, besides many

wounded', though this total seems too high. National Archives (London), Foreign Office, *Portugal: Annual Reports for 1914 to 1918*, p 28.

13. Ana Mira (ed), *Actas das Sessões Secretas da Câmara dos Deputados e do Senado da República Sobre a Participação de Portugal na I Grande Guerra* (Assembleia da República/Afrontamento, Lisbon: 2002) p 62.

14. *Ibid*, p 116.

15. *O Século* (Lisbon), 2 August 1917.

16. *Portugal na Primeira Guerra Mundial (1914–1918)*, Vol 2, *As Negociações Diplomáticas e a Acção Militar na Europa e em África* (Ministério dos Negócios Estrangeiros, Lisbon: 1997) pp 202–3.

17. *Diário da Câmara dos Deputados*, 1 August 1918. This document and the one that follows it were part of a series of telegrams read out by Amílcar Mota, at the time Secretary of State for War, with the intention of demonstrating the mistakes made in the organization of the CEP. The impression made was considerable.

18. Norton de Matos, *Memórias e Trabalhos da Minha Vida*, Vol 3 (Editora Marítimo-Colonial, Lisbon: 1944) p 38.

19. Tamagnini de Abreu's plight and the consequences of political infighting on the CEP's existence are laid bare in Isabel Pestana Marques (ed), *Memórias do General, 1915–1919: 'Os Meus Três Comandos' de Fernando Tamagnini* (Fundação Mariana Seixas, Viseu: 2004).

20. João Chagas, *Diário*, Vol 3, *1918*, pp 47–9.

21. Arquivo Nacional (Lisbon), Ministério do Interior, Direcção-Geral da Administração Política e Civil, stack 67 (1917), letter, 26 November 1917, administrator

of the municipality of Lamego to the Civil Governor of Viseu. The civil governor requested, and received, military reinforcements on the basis of this letter.

22. Ministère des Affaires Etrangères (MAE), Paris, Guerre 1914–1918, Portugal, Dossier Général, 635, telegram, Lisbon, 26 November 1917, Emile Daeschner to the MAE.

23. *O Mundo* (Lisbon), 31 May 1921.

24. Much was made in the press, in the days that followed, about the nature of this arrest; it was generally believed that Costa had hidden in the hotel when the army began to search the premises, being found eventually in a kitchen lift.

25. *Diário de Notícias* (Lisbon), 18 December 1917.

4 Waiting in the wings, 1918–1919

1. Fundação Mário Soares (FMS), Documentos Afonso Costa (DAC), 'Horas de provação para amigos e inimigos', Forte da Graça, 12 January 1918.

2. FMS, DAC, letter, Forte da Graça, 28 January 1918, Afonso Costa to Germano Martins.

3. FMS, DAC, letter, Forte da Graça, 28 January 1918, Afonso Costa to Germano Martins.

4. João Chagas, *Diário*, Vol 3, *1918*, p 72.

5. António José de Almeida, 'Os presos políticos', in *República* (Lisbon), 9 March 1918; reproduced in Marques (ed), *Afonso Costa*, pp 172–4.

6. His daughter Maria Emília would marry Fernando de Castro, a lawyer who would go on to become an important part of the Costa clan, participating in his father-in-law's political and professional activities.

7. João Chagas, *Diário*, Vol 3, *1918*, pp 65–6.

8. Armando Malheiro da Silva, *Sidónio e Sidonismo, Vol 2 História de um Caso Político* (Imprensa da Universidade de Coimbra, Coimbra: 2006) pp 36–58.

9. António Ferro, 'O Assassino da Pátria', in *O Jornal* (Lisbon), 20 November 1919, reproduced in Ernesto Castro Leal, *António Ferro: Espaço Politico e Imaginário Social (1918–1932)* (Edições Cosmos, Lisbon: 1994) pp 232–5.

10. See Arquivo Histórico Diplomático (AHD), L 591-A, Sala, for the minute of the first meeting, held on 27 November 1918 and chaired by Sidónio Pais, to discuss Portugal's strategy at the forthcoming peace negotiations.

11. FMS, DAC, letter, Paris, 18 December 1918, Afonso Costa to Maria Emília Barros Abreu Costa.

12. FMS, DAC, 'Apontamento de 1 a 5 de Janeiro de 1919' (from the MacMahon).

13. AHD, Third Floor, Armário [A] 6, Maço [M] 37, telegram, Paris, 21 December 1918, Egas Moniz to the President of the Republic, Lisbon.

14. AHD, Third Floor, A6, M19, telegram, Paris, 17 January 1919, Egas Moniz to Ministry of Foreign Affairs.

15. AHD, Third Floor, A6, M19, telegram, Paris, 8 January 1919, Egas Moniz to Ministry of Foreign Affairs.

16. AHD, Third Floor, A6, M19, original English-language version of memorandum distributed to Balfour, Lansing, Pichon, Sonnino and Matsui.

17. AHD, Third Floor, A6, M19, letter, Paris, 15 January 1919, Arthur J Balfour to Egas Moniz. Apart from the main Powers, only Brazil had more delegates than Portugal, and this was because of Woodrow Wilson's

insistence, not because of the country's role in the conflict.

18. AHD, Third Floor, A6, M37, telegram, Lisbon, 31 January 1919, Minister of Foreign Affairs *ad interim* to Egas Moniz.

19. AHD, Third Floor, A6, M19, telegram, Paris, 28 February 1919, Egas Moniz to the Minister of Foreign Affairs *ad interim*.

20. AHD, Third Floor, A6, M19, telegram, Paris, 28 February 1919, Egas Moniz to the President of the Republic.

5 Negotiating the Treaty

1. Reprinted in Marques (ed), *Afonso Costa*, pp 413–4.

2. FMS, DAC, letter, Paris, 5 March 1919, Alzira Costa to Maria Emília Barros Abreu Costa.

3. *Diário de Notícias* (Lisbon), 8 March 1919.

4. AHD, Third Floor, A6, M17, telegram, Lisbon, 16 March 1919, President of the Republic to Egas Moniz.

5. Domingos Leite Pereira headed a cabinet, made up of Democrats and Evolutionists, which had been purged of 'New' Republicans.

6. AHD, Third Floor, A6, M37, telegram, Paris, 1 April 1919, Afonso Costa to the Prime Minister.

7. AHD, Third Floor, A9, M6B, telegram, Paris, 20 March 1919, Afonso Costa to the Minister of Foreign Affairs.

8. AHD, Third Floor, A9, M6B, 'Conferência que teve lugar no Hotel Majestic no dia 21 de Abril de 1919'.

9. AHD, A9, M6B, telegram, Paris, 26 April 1919, Afonso Costa to the Minister of Foreign Affairs.

10. AHD, L 591-A, Sala, minutes of the meeting of the Portuguese delegation to the Peace Conference, 22 April 1919.

11. AHD, Third Floor, A6, M23, telegram, Lisbon, 6 April, Minister of Foreign Affairs to Afonso Costa.

12. *O Século* (Lisbon), 9 April 1919.

13. AHD, Third Floor, A6, M23, telegram, Paris, 12 April 1919, Afonso Costa to the Minister of the Navy.

14. AHD, Third Floor, A6 M19, 'Resumo das declarações feitas pelo Snr Loucheur em nome do Comité dos Quatro na Reunião para que ontem às 9 da noite convocou o Coronel Freire d'Andrade'.

15. The minutes of the Portuguese Delegation's meetings make clear that Costa and his collaborators saw the text of the Treaty as a defeat. Teixeira Gomes stated that he would 'resign my mandate as a Portuguese Minister should we have to sign an unchanged Treaty.' João Chagas urged his colleagues to be calm and to consider, collectively, the following question: 'Should we sign a Treaty which does not afford us any moral right and which harms us materially?' Batalha Reis, a career diplomat, was the most pessimistic of all; for him, the Treaty represented Portugal's greatest defeat since the battle of Ksar El Kebir, in 1578, which had paved the way for the loss of independence to Spain.

16. AHD Third Floor, A6 M20, 'Discurso do Dr Afonso Costa na Sessão Plenária das Preliminares da Paz de 6 de Maio de 1919'.

17. José Medeiros Ferreira, *Portugal na Conferência da Paz: Paris, 1919* (Quetzal, Lisbon: 1992) p 48.

18. AHD, Third Floor, A6, M20, telegram, Lisbon, 11 May 1919, Minister of Foreign Affairs to Afonso Costa.

19. AHD, Third Floor, A6, M20, telegram, Paris, 12 May 1919, Afonso Costa to the Minister of Foreign Affairs.

20. AHD, Third Floor A6, M20, telegram, Paris, 16 May 1919, Afonso Costa to the Minister of Foreign Affairs.

21. AHD, A6, M44, telegram, Lisbon, 17 May 1919, Magalhães Lima, Ferreira Pinharanda, Boto Machado and Pinheiro Belo to Afonso Costa.

22. AHD, Third Floor, A6, M20, telegram, Paris, 7 May 1919, Afonso Costa to the Minister of Foreign Affairs.

23. AHD, Third Floor, A6, M20, telegram, Lisbon, 23 June 1919, Minister of Foreign Affairs to Afonso Costa.

6 Domestic Reaction and Ratification

1. AHD, Third Floor, A6, M20, telegram, Lisbon, 30 June 1919, President of the Republic to Afonso Costa.

2. AHD, Third Floor, A6, M23, telegram, Lisbon, 6 December 1919, Minister of Foreign Affairs to Afonso Costa.

3. AHD, Third Floor, A6, M23, telegram, Paris, 9 December 1919, Afonso Costa to the Minister of Foreign Affairs.

4. AHD, Third Floor, A6, M23, letter, Paris, 10 December 1919, Sécrétariat Général de la Conférence de la Paix to the Portuguese delegation.

5. AHD, Third Floor, A6, M23, telegram, Paris, 20 April 1920, Afonso Costa to the Minister of Foreign Affairs.

6. AHD, Third Floor, A11, M20, telegram, Paris, 1 July 1919, Afonso Costa to the Minister of Foreign Affairs.

7. AHD, Third Floor, A6, M20, telegram, Lisbon, 11 August 1919, Minister of Foreign Affairs to Afonso Cota.

8. AHD, Third Floor A1, M610, telegram, Paris, 12 October 1919, Afonso Costa to the Portuguese Legation in London.

9. AHD, Third Floor, A6, M20, telegram, Paris, 22 October 1919, Afonso Costa to the Minister of Foreign Affairs.

10. AHD, Third Floor, A6, M20, telegram, Paris, 17 December 1919, Afonso Costa to the Minister of Foreign Affairs.

11. AHD, Third Floor, A6, M20, telegram, Lisbon, 20 December 1919, Minister of Foreign Affairs to Afonso Costa.

12. AHD, Third Floor, A6, M20, telegram, Paris, 5 January 1920, Afonso Costa to the Minister of Foreign Affairs.

13. AHD, Third Floor, A6, M20, telegram, Lisbon, 8 January 1920, Minister of Foreign Affairs to Afonso Costa.

14. AHD, Third Floor, A6, M20, telegram, Lisbon, 13 January 1920, Minister of Foreign Affairs to Afonso Costa.

15. AHD, Third Floor, A6, M20, telegram, Paris, 24 January 1920, Afonso Costa to the Minister of Foreign Affairs.

16. AHD, Third Floor, A6, M20, telegram, Lisbon, 31 January 1920, Minister of Foreign Affairs to Afonso Costa.

17. AHD, Third Floor, A6, M20, telegram, Paris, 18 February 1920, Afonso Costa to the Minister of Foreign Affairs.

18. AHD, Third Floor, A11, M20, telegram, Paris, 23 February 1920, Afonso Costa to the Minister of Foreign Affairs.

19. AHD, Third Floor, A6, M20, telegram, Paris, 23 February 1920, Afonso Costa to the Minister of Foreign Affairs.

20. AHD, Third Floor, A6, M20, letter, Paris, 16 March 1920, Afonso Costa to the Minister of Foreign Affairs.

21. The eight-man body was evenly split between Democrats and Liberals, and included party leaders António Granjo and António Maria da Silva.

22. *Diário da Câmara dos Deputados*, 30 March 1920, p 33.

23. *O Mundo* (Lisbon), 31 March 1920.

24. *O Mundo* (Lisbon), 2 April 1920.

7 Undoing the Treaty

1. He was completely wrong. Milner's outrage was expressed in a memorandum dated 29 May: 'The Portuguese have in my opinion no claim whatever to receive a mandate for any portion of German East Africa as the share of what they have done in the conquest of it [...] They even failed to defend their own boundaries against von Lettow[-Vorbeck], when our operations rendered his position in East Africa untenable, and by that failure prolonged the war in East Africa for about a year.' Milner memorandum, 29 May 1919, Milner Papers, cited by William Roger Louis, 'Great Britain and the African Peace Settlement of 1919', in *American Historical Review*, Vol 71 (1966) p 889.

2. AHD, Third Floor, A9, M6B, 'Conferência de 12 de Julho de 1919'.

3. AHD, Third Floor, A9, M6B, letter, Paris, 27 September 1919, Afonso Costa to the Minister of Foreign Affairs.

4. AHD, Third Floor, A6, M19, letter, Paris, 30 January 1920, Sir John Bradbury, British Delegate to the Reparations Commission, to Afonso Costa.

5. AHD, Third Floor, A11, M20, letter, Paris, 18 March 1920, Afonso Costa to the Minister of Foreign Affairs.

6. AHD, Third Floor, A11, M20, letter, Paris, 14 April 1920, Afonso Costa to the Portuguese minister in Switzerland (Bartolomeu Ferreira). He had already attempted, in January 1920, to interest the Supreme Council in this matter, but the request had been turned down, perhaps, Costa believed, because the treaty had not been ratified.

7. Telegram from Sir Eyre Crowe to Lord Derby, in Paris, on 3 May 1920, a copy of which Teixeira Gomes sent Costa. AHD, Third Floor, A11, M20; AHD, Third Floor, A11, M20, letter, Paris, 5 May 1920, Jules Cambon to Afonso Costa.

8. AHD, Third Floor, A11, M20, letter, Paris, 8 May 1920, Afonso Costa to the Portuguese minister in London.

9. AHD, Third Floor, A11, M20, telegram, Paris, 25 April 1920, Afonso Costa to the Minister of Foreign Affairs.

10. AHD, Third Floor, A11, M20, '*Mémoire des reclamations introduites par le Portugal pour la reparation des dommages qui lui ont été causes par l'Allemagne et prévus à l'annexe I de la Partie VIII du Traité de Paix de Versailles*'.

11. *Diário de Notícias* (Lisbon), 5 June 1920.

12. AHD, Third Floor, A11, M20, letter, Paris, 24 May 1920, Teixeira Gomes to Sir Eyre Crowe.

13. AHD, Third Floor, A11, M20, telegram, Paris, 24 May 1920, Afonso Costa to the Minister of Foreign Affairs.

14. AHD, Third Floor, A11, M20, letter, Paris, 27 May 1920, John Bradbury to Afonso Costa.
15. AHD, Third Floor, A11, M20, letter, Paris, 28 May 1920, Afonso Costa to Sir John Bradbury.
16. *The Times* (London), 1 June 1920.
17. AHD, Third Floor, A6, M37, letter, Paris, 15 June 1920, Afonso Costa to the Minister of Foreign Affairs.
18. FMS, DAC, letter, Paris, 1 June 1920, Afonso Costa to Maria Emília Barros Abreu Costa.
19. AHD, Third Floor, A11, M20, letter, London, 5 June 1920, Lancelot Oilphant to the British Secretary, Reparations Commission, Hotel Astoria, Paris.
20. AHD, Third Floor, A6, M37, telegram, Lisbon, 12 June 1920, António José de Almeida to Afonso Costa.
21. FMS, DAC, letter, Soisson, 15 June 1920, Afonso Costa to Maria Emília Barros Abreu Costa.
22. AHD, Third Floor, A11, M20, telegram, Paris, 27 June 1920, Afonso Costa to the Portuguese legation in London.
23. *Diário de Notícias*, 10 July 1920.
24. FMS, DAC, letter, Spa, 9 July 1920, Afonso Costa to Maria Emília Barros Abreu Costa.
25. FMS, DAC, letter, Spa, 5 July 1920, Afonso Costa to Maria Emília Barros Abreu Costa.
26. FMS, DAC, letter, Spa, 13 July 1920, Afonso Costa to Maria Emília Barros Abreu Costa.
27. FMS, DAC, letter, Spa, 15 July 1920, Afonso Costa to Maria Emília Barros Abreu Costa.
28. FMS, DAC, letter, Spa, 17 July 1920, Afonso Costa to Maria Emília Barros Abreu Costa.
29. AHD, Third Floor, A6, M17, telegram, Paris, 20 July 1920, Afonso Costa to the Minister of Foreign Affairs.

30. *Diário de Notícias* (Lisbon), 18 October 1920.
31. In its coverage of the event, on 30 September 1920, *Le Temps* (Paris) stressed the German delegate's speech and the favourable impression it created, omitting to mention Costa's impassioned words. The same was true of *The Times* (London), whose correspondent wrote, 'Herr Bergmann's speech made a good impression on the Conference, and was received with loud applause'; *The Times* (London), 29 September 1920.

8 Between Paris and Lisbon

1. AHD, Third Floor, A6 M37, telegram, Paris, 19 June 1919, Afonso Costa to the President of the Chamber of Deputies.
2. *O Mundo* (Lisbon), 28 July 1920.
3. *Diário de Notícias* (Lisbon), 17 August 1920.
4. See *Le Temps* (Paris), 3 December 1920, for a better account of events than that provided by *The Times* (London) of the same date.
5. FMS, DAC, telegram, Nice, 26 February 1921, Afonso Costa to Maria Emília Barros Abreu Costa.
6. FMS, DAC, letter, Paris, 9 March 1921, Afonso Costa to Maria Emília Barros Abreu Costa. It was in *O Norte* that the articles about Costa's experiences in December 1917 were first published, being reprinted in Lisbon's *O Mundo*.
7. *O Século* (Lisbon), 8 April 1921.
8. The briefest of descriptions can be found in *The Times* (London), 11 April 1921.
9. *O Século* (Lisbon), 11 April 1921.
10. *Diário da Câmara dos Deputados* (Lisbon), 24 August 1921.

11. *Diário da Câmara dos Deputados* (Lisbon), 24 August 1921.

12. *Diário de Notícias* (Lisbon), 15 September 1921. Reprinted *verbatim* in *O Mundo* (Lisbon), 16 September 1921.

13. FMS, DAC, letter, Paris, 23 October 1921, Afonso Costa to Maria Emília Barros Abreu Costa.

14. FMS, DAC, letter, Paris, 28 October 1921, Afonso Costa to Maria Emília Barros Abreu Costa.

15. FMS, DAC, letter, Paris, 30 October 1921, Afonso Costa to Maria Emília Barros Abreu Costa.

16. Álvaro de Castro would quit the Nationalist Party as a result of the crisis, forming yet another political force, known as 'Republican Action'.

17. *O Século* (Lisbon), 10 November 1923.

18. *O Século* (Lisbon), 10 November 1923. A 'conto' was an informal term for 1,000 escudos.

19. Afonso Costa quotes part of this letter in FMS, DAC, letter, Paris, 3 March 1924, Afonso Costa to Maria Emília Barros Abreu Costa.

20. *O Libertador* (Lisbon), 14 June 1925.

21. FMS, DAC, letter, Geneva, 11 March 1926, Afonso Costa to Maria Emília Barros Abreu Costa.

22. FMS, DAC, letter, Paris, 8 May 1935, Afonso Costa to Maria Emília Barros Abreu Costa.

23. FMS, DAC, letter, Madrid, 23 April 1931, Afonso Costa to Maria Emília Barros Abreu Costa.

24. *Legislação Repressiva e Antidemocrática do Regime Fascista* (Presidência do Conselho de Ministros/ Comissão do Livro Negro Sobre o Regime Fascista, Lisbon: 1985) pp 130–4.

25. *Diário da Manhã* (Lisbon), 27 November 1932. In a private letter, Afonso Costa explained that the *Diário de Notícias* had printed roughly a quarter of what he had said, leaving out issues such as finance, the on-going reform of the Constitution, poverty and possible solutions for all of these problems. FMS, DAC, letter, Paris, 28 November 1932, Afonso Costa to Maria Emília Barros Abreu Costa.

26. *Diário da Manhã* (Lisbon), 24 March 1935.

27. FMS, DAC, letter, Paris, 4 September 1936, Afonso Costa to Maria Emília Barros Abreu Costa.

28. *Diário da Manhã* (Lisbon), 29 November 1932.

29. FMS, DAC, letter, Antwerp, 20 February 1936, Afonso Costa to Maria Emília Barros Abreu Costa.

30. *Arbitrage entre le Portugal et l'Allemagne: Sentence aribtrale du 31 Juillet 1928 concernant la responsabilité de l'Allemagne à raison des dommages causes dans les colonies portugaises du Sud de l'Afrique* (Imprimerie de la Société de la Gazette de Lausanne et Journal Suisse, Lausanne: 1928).

31. *Arbitrage entre le Portugal et l'Allemagne,* p 68.

32. 'Declarações do Sr. Dr. Oliveira Salazar' in *Diário da Manhã* (Lisbon), 21 October 1933. The interview was originally published in the *Diário de Notícias* (Lisbon), 20 October 1933.

33. *Entrevista Complementar do Doutor Afonso Costa com a Resposta a Salazar* (transcribed from *Portugal Republicano*, Rio de Janeiro: n.d.).

34. *Diário da Manhã* (Lisbon), 29 May 1966.

Chronology

YEAR	AGE	THE LIFE AND THE LAND
1871	0	6 Mar: Afonso Costa born in Seia.
		Prime Minister Fontes Pereira de Melo inaugurates the 'Regeneration', a period of political calm and material progress. The 'Casino Conferences' mark the beginning of a new literary and cultural age in Portugal.
1880	9	National demonstrations mark the 300th anniversary of the death of Luís de Camões, Portugal's national poet.
1883	12	Costa enters secondary school.
1884	13	Start of the Berlin Conference, which limits Portuguese sovereignty in the Congo region.
		Hermengildo Capelo and Roberto Ivens set off on their overland crossing of Africa, linking Angola to Mozambique and laying claim to the territory in between.
1887	16	Costa enrols at the University of Coimbra.

YEAR	HISTORY	CULTURE
1871	Franco-Prussian War: Wilhelm I of Prussia declared German Emperor at Versailles; capitulation of Paris; Treaty of Frankfurt ends war, ceding Alsace-Lorraine to Germany. Commune in Paris. Britain annexes Kimberley diamond fields in South Africa.	Lewis Carroll, *Through the Looking Glass.* George Eliot, *Middlemarch.* Charles Darwin, *The Descent of Man.* Verdi, *Aïda.*
1880	France annexes Tahiti. Transvaal Republic declares independence from Britain. Pacific War: Chile vs Bolivia and Peru (–1884).	Death of George Eliot. Dostoevsky, *The Brothers Karamazov.* Rodin, *The Thinker.*
1883	British decide to evacuate the Sudan. The Orient Express makes its first run.	Death of Wagner. Nietzsche, *Thus Spake Zarathustra.*
1884	General Gordon arrives in Khartoum. Germans occupy South-West Africa. Gold discovered in the Transvaal.	Mark Twain, *Huckleberry Finn.* *Oxford English Dictionary* begins publication (–1928). Seurat, *Une Baignade à Asnières.*
1887	First Colonial Conference in London. Queen Victoria's Golden Jubilee.	Arthur Conan Doyle, *A Study in Scarlet.* Verdi, *Otello.* Van Gogh, *Moulin de la Galette.*

YEAR	AGE	THE LIFE AND THE LAND
1889	18	António de Oliveira Salazar born in Vimieiro. *Dom* Luís dies and is succeeded by *Dom* Carlos.
1890	19	British ultimatum over the division of southern Africa provokes patriotic backlash and political instability.
		Costa becomes active in republican politics, publishing *Ultimatum*, with António José de Almeida.
1891	20	Republican rising in Oporto. Portuguese government defaults on foreign loans.
		Treaty with Great Britain settles Mozambican borders.
1892	21	Afonso Costa marries Alzira de Barros Abreu.
1894	23	Costa concludes his degree; his first son, Sebastião, is born.
		Regenerationist leader Hintze Ribeiro begins to govern 'in dictatorship' (with parliament closed).
		Beginning of campaigns to pacify southern Mozambique.

YEAR	HISTORY	CULTURE
1889	Austro-Hungarian Crown Prince Rudolf commits suicide at Mayerling. London Dock Strike.	Jerome K Jerome, *Three Men in a Boat*. Richard Strauss, *Don Juan*.
1890	Bismarck dismissed by Wilhelm II. Britain exchanges Heligoland with Germany for Zanzibar and Pemba. First general election in Japan. German Social Democrats adopt Marxist Erfurt Programme.	Oscar Wilde, *The Picture of Dorian Gray*. Mascagni, *Cavelleria Rusticana*. First moving picture shows in New York.
1891	Triple Alliance (Austria-Hungary, Germany, Italy) renewed for 12 years. Franco-Russian entente. Young Turk Movement founded in Vienna.	Thomas Hardy, *Tess of the D'Urbervilles*. Mahler, *Symphony No 1*. Toulouse-Lautrec produces his first music-hall posters.
1892	Britain and Germany agree on Cameroon. Pan-Slav Conference in Cracow.	Bernard Shaw, *Mrs Warren's Profession*. Tchaikovsky, *The Nutcracker*.
1894	Sino-Japanese War begins: Japanese defeat Chinese at Port Arthur. Dreyfus Case begins in France.	G & W Grossmith, *The Diary of a Nobody*. Anthony Hope, *The Prisoner of Zenda*.

YEAR	AGE	THE LIFE AND THE LAND
1895	24	Afonso Costa concludes his doctorate and establishes a legal office in Coimbra.
		Ngungunhane, Emperor of Gaza, is arrested by Captain Mouzinho de Albuquerque.
1896	25	Costa joins the lecturing staff at the University of Coimbra. A daughter, Maria Emília, is born.
1898	27	Costa begins a cure for tuberculosis in Davos-Platz.
1899	28	Costa is awarded the Chair of Judiciary Organization and is elected to parliament by the city of Oporto.
1900	29	Election is re-run, but Costa retains his seat. A second son, Afonso, is born.

YEAR	HISTORY	CULTURE
1895	Sino-Japanese War ends. Armenians massacred in Ottoman Empire. Jameson Raid into Transvaal. Cuba rebels against Spanish rule. Marconi invents radio telegraphy.	H G Wells, *The Time Machine*. W B Yeats, *Poems*. Tchaikovsky, *Swan Lake*.
1896	Failure of Jameson Raid: Kaiser Wilhelm II sends 'Kruger Telegram'. Kitchener begins reconquest of the Sudan. Russia and China sign Manchurian Convention. Klondike Gold Rush.	Chekhov, *The Seagull*. Richard Strauss, *Also Spracht Zarathustra*. Puccini, *La Bohème*. Nobel Prizes established.
1898	Dreyfus case: Zola publishes *J'Accuse* letter. Spanish-American War: US gains Cuba, Puerto Rico, Guam and the Philippines.	Thomas Hardy, *Wessex Poems*. Henry James, *The Turn of the Screw*. Oscar Wilde, *The Ballad of Reading Gaol*.
1899	Anglo-Egyptian Sudan Convention. Outbreak of Second Boer War. First Peace Conference at the Hague.	Rudyard Kipling, *Stalky and Co*. Pinero, *Trelawny of the Wells*. Elgar, *Enigma Variations*.
1900	Second Boer War: relief of Mafeking. Assassination of King Umberto I of Italy. Boxer Rising in China.	Freud, *The Interpretation of Dreams*. Puccini, *Tosca*. Joseph Conrad, *Lord Jim*.

YEAR	AGE	THE LIFE AND THE LAND
1902	31	Mouzinho de Albuquerque commits suicide, putting an end to the possibility of a militarisation of Portuguese politics.
1903	32	Edward VII visits Portugal.
		João Franco, a former Regenerationist minister, launches his Liberal-Regenerationist Party, promising a new era in Portuguese politics.
1906	35	Afonso Costa's third son, Fernando, is born. Costa is elected to the Directorate, the highest executive body of the Portuguese Republican Party, and to Parliament by the city of Lisbon. His violent speeches on the advances question lead to a month's suspension.
		Dom Carlos turns to João Franco to form a government. Reasonably fair elections result in a split chamber, and Franco admits the practice of advances on the Civil List.

YEAR	HISTORY	CULTURE
1902	Anglo-Japanese treaty recognises the independence of China and Korea. Treaty of Vereenigung ends Boer War. Triple Alliance between Austria, Germany and Italy renewed for another six years. USA acquires perpetual control over Panama Canal.	Arthur Conan Doyle, *The Hound of the Baskervilles*. Anton Chekhov, *Three Sisters*. Monet, *Waterloo Bridge*. Elgar, *Pomp and Circumstance March No 1*.
1903	King Alexander I of Serbia murdered. King Edward VII visits Paris and French President Loubet visits London – beginning of Entente Cordiale. Wright Brothers' first flight.	Henry James, *The Ambassadors*. George Bernard Shaw, *Man and Superman*. Jack London, *The Call of the Wild*. Bruckner, *Symphony No. 9*.
1906	Edward VII of England and Kaiser Wilhelm II of Germany meet. Britain grants self-government to Transvaal and Orange River Colonies. British ultimatum forces Turkey to cede Sinai Peninsula to Egypt. Armand Fallieres elected President of France. In France, Dreyfus rehabilitated. Major earthquake in San Francisco USA kills over 1,000.	John Galsworthy, *A Man of Property*. O Henry, *The Four Million*. Foundation of Everyman's Library by Edward Dent. Andre Derain, *Port of London*. Massenet, *Ariane*. Invention of first jukebox.

YEAR	AGE	THE LIFE AND THE LAND
1907	36	Costa quits the Directorate. João Franco is allowed to govern 'in dictatorship'.
1908	37	*Dom* Carlos and crown-prince *Dom* Luís Filipe are murdered in Lisbon. *Dom* Manuel II is crowned king. Costa is arrested as part of a government crackdown against an imminent republican revolt, and is later elected to Parliament by Lisbon; intense parliamentary activity follows.
1910	39	5 Oct: The Portuguese monarchy is overthrown and a republic is proclaimed. Costa is elected to parliament by Lisbon, and undergoes a cure in Cauterets. Later forms part of Provisional Government as Minister of Justice, and establishes himself as the most active minister.

YEAR	HISTORY	CULTURE
1907	British and French agree on Siamese independence.	Joseph Conrad, *The Secret Agent*.
	Dominion status granted to New Zealand.	Maxim Gorky, *Mother*.
		R M Rilke, *Neue Gedichte*.
	Rasputin gains influence at the court of Tsar Nicholas II.	First Cubist exhibition in Paris.
		Edvard Munch, *Amor and Psyche*.
1908	Union of South Africa is established.	E M Forster, *A Room with a View*.
	Ferdinand I declares Bulgaria's independence and assumes the title of Tsar.	Kenneth Grahame, *The Wind in the Willows*.
		Anatole France, *Penguin Island*.
		Marc Chagall, *Nu Rouge*.
		Maurice de Vlaminck, *The Red Trees*.
		Bela Bartok, *String Quartet No. 1*.
		Elgar, *Symphony No. 1 in A-Flat*.
1910	King Edward VII dies; succeeded by George V.	E M Forster, *Howard's End*.
	Egyptian Premier Butros Ghali assassinated.	H G Wells, *The History of Mr. Polly*.
		Karl May, *Winnetou*.
	South Africa becomes a dominion within the British Empire with Botha as Premier.	Modigliani, *The Cellist*.
		Elgar, *Concerto for Violin in B Minor, Op. 61*.
	Portugal is proclaimed a republic.	Puccini, *La Fanciulla del West*.
	Marie Curie publishes *Treatise on Radiography*.	R Vaughan Williams, *Sea Symphony*.

YEAR	AGE	THE LIFE AND THE LAND
1911	40	Tension with the Catholic Church grows as Costa's separation of Church and State is enacted. Costa falls gravely ill, but is elected to the Constituent Assembly by Lisbon. He resumes academic life, securing a Chair at Lisbon's Escola Politécnica.
		The Republic's constitution is promulgated and Manuel de Arriaga is elected President. João Chagas is appointed Prime Minister, and the Portuguese Republican Party's (PRP) unity is shattered.
		Costa heads the Democratic Parliamentary Faction.
1912	41	PRP splits into three factions; successive weak governments fail to provide stability.
1913	42	Costa forms his first government, serving as Prime Minister and Minister of Finance; later, he is named Director of the Law Faculty of the new University of Lisbon.
1914	43	Costa is forced to resign, and Bernardino Machado becomes Prime Minister. Costa becomes a leading interventionist figure once war breaks out in Europe.
		Portugal is invited to join Allies but is prevented from doing so by its military weakness; a German incursion provokes chaos in southern Angola.

YEAR	HISTORY	CULTURE
1911	Arrival of German gunboat *Panther* in Agadir triggers international crisis. Peter Stolypyn, Russian Premier, assassinated. Italy declares war on Turkey.	Cubism becomes public phenomenon in Paris. Max Beerbohm, *Zuleika Dobson*. D H Lawrence, *The White Peacock*. Saki, *The Chronicles of Clovis*. George Bracque, *Man with a Guitar*. Strauss, *Der Rosenkavalier*. Stravinsky, *Petrushka*.
1912	*Titanic* sinks. Woodrow Wilson is elected US President. Armistice between Turkey, Bulgaria, Serbia and Montenegro. Lenin establishes connection with Stalin and takes over editorship of *Pravda*.	Alfred Adler, *The Nervous Character*. C G Jung, *The Theory of Psychoanalysis*. Marcel Duchamp, *Nude descending a staircase II*. Schoenberg, *Pierrot Lunaire*. Ravel, *Daphnis and Chloe*.
1913	Bulgarians renew Turkish War. King George I of Greece assassinated and succeeded by Constantine I. Second Balkan war breaks out. US Federal Reserve System is established.	D H Lawrence, *Sons and Lovers*. Thomas Mann, *Death in Venice*. Marcel Proust, *Du côté de chez Swann*. Igor Stravinsky, *Le Sacre du Printemps*.
1914	Archduke Franz Ferdinand of Austria-Hungary and his wife are assassinated in Sarajevo. Outbreak of First World War: Battles of Mons, the Marne and First Ypres, Tannenberg and Masurian Lakes.	James Joyce, *Dubliners*. Theodore Dreiser, *The Titan*. Gustav Holst, *The Planets*. Matisse, *The Red Studio*. Braque, *Music*. Film: Charlie Chaplin in *Making a Living*.

YEAR	AGE	THE LIFE AND THE LAND
1915	44	Manuel de Arriaga asks General Pimenta de Castro to form a government to oversee elections.
		14 May: Pimenta de Castro overthrown by a violent revolt; PRP emerges from elections in control of both chambers.
		Costa is elected to the Chamber of Deputies by Lisbon.
		Nov: Costa forms his second government, keeping the Finance portfolio.
1916	45	The Costa-led Portuguese government seizes German ships interned in its harbours.
		10 Mar: Germany declares war. Costa keeps the Finance portfolio in the first 'Sacred Union' cabinet.
		A Portuguese division undergoes intensive training at Tancos. Military expeditions are dispatched to Africa, but defeat follows at Newala (German East Africa).
1917	46	The Portuguese Expeditionary Corps (CEP) is dispatched to the Western Front.
		The first 'Sacred Union' cabinet falls in confusing circumstances; strikes and food riots break out all over Portugal as a result of worsening economic situation. Costa heads his third government, still under the label of the 'Sacred Union'; accompanies President Bernardino Machado to France and Great Britain; returns to Paris to attend Inter-Allied Conference; is arrested in Oporto and then sent to Elvas, where he is kept incommunicado.
		Sidónio Pais overthrows the government and unveils his 'New Republic'.

YEAR	HISTORY	CULTURE
1915	First World War: Battles of Neuve Chappelle and Loos. The 'Shells Scandal'. Germans sink the British liner *Lusitania,* killing 1,198.	Joseph Conrad, *Victory.* John Buchan, *The Thirty-Nine Steps.* Ezra Pound, *Cathay.* Film: *The Birth of a Nation.*
1916	First World War. Western Front: Battle of Verdun, France. The Battle of the Somme. The Battle of Jutland. US President Woodrow Wilson is re-elected. Wilson issues Peace Note to belligerents in European war. Lloyd George becomes Prime Minister.	James Joyce, *Portrait of an Artist as a Young Man.* Film: *Intolerance.*
1917	First World War. February Revolution in Russia. Battle of Passchendaele (Third Ypres). British and Commonwealth forces take Jerusalem. USA declares war on Germany. Balfour Declaration favouring the establishment of a national home for the Jewish People in Palestine. China declares war on Germany and Russia. German and Russian delegates sign armistice at Brest-Litovsk.	P G Wodehouse, *The Man With Two Left Feet.* T S Eliot, *Prufrock and Other Observations.* Leon Feuchtwanger, *Jud Suess.* Piet Mondrian launches *De Stijl* magazine in Holland. Picasso designs 'surrealist' costumes and set for Satie's *Parade.* Hans Pfitzner, *Palestrina.* Prokofiev, *Classical Symphony.* Film: *Easy Street.*

YEAR	AGE	THE LIFE AND THE LAND
1918	47	9 Apr: The CEP is obliterated by the German army and little is done to rebuild it.
		May: Costa leaves Portugal for Paris. Egas Moniz is named Portuguese representative at the Paris Peace Conference.
		Dec: Sidónio Pais is murdered.
1919	48	Political chaos is aggravated by a monarchist rebellion which takes control of the north of Portugal, including Oporto; brief civil war sees Republicans emerge triumphant.
		Costa renounces political activity; despite this, he is elected to the Chamber of Deputies, but does not take up his seat. He is also elected to the PRP's Directorate, again refusing to participate in proceedings.
		Mar: Costa takes control of the Portuguese delegation to the Paris Peace Conference, and signs Treaty of Versailles.
		The CEP's remnants return from France.
		The PRP is again in control of parliament, and António José de Almeida is elected President.
		25 Sep: the Supreme Council recognizes Portugal's right to Kionga.
1920	49	PRP, caught up in a violent power struggle, splits again.
		1 April: Portugal ratifies Treaty of Versailles.
		Costa takes part in the Spa conference, and represents Portugal at the League of Nations, where he is elected vice-president of its Third Commission.

YEAR	HISTORY	CULTURE
1918	First World War ends.	Alexander Blok, *The Twelve*.
	Ex-Tsar Nicholas II and family executed.	Gerald Manley Hopkins, *Poems*.
	Armistice signed between Allies and Germany; German Fleet surrenders.	Luigi Pirandello, *Six Characters in Search of an Author*.
		Bela Bartok, *Bluebeard's Castle*.
	Kaiser Wilhelm II of Germany abdicates.	Puccini, *Il Trittico*.
		Edvard Munch, *Bathing Man*.
1919	Communist Revolt in Berlin.	Bauhaus movement founded by Walter Gropius.
	Paris Peace Conference adopts principle of founding League of Nations.	Thomas Hardy, *Collected Poems*.
	Benito Mussolini founds fascist movement in Italy.	George Bernard Shaw, *Heartbreak House*.
	Irish War of Independence begins.	Film: *The Cabinet of Dr Caligari*.
	US Senate votes against ratification of Treaty of Versailles, leaving the USA outside the League of Nations.	
1920	League of Nations comes into existence.	F Scott Fitzgerald, *This Side of Paradise*.
	The Hague is selected as seat of International Court of Justice.	Franz Kafka, *The Country Doctor*.
	Bolsheviks win Russian Civil War.	Katherine Mansfield, *Bliss*.
		Rambert School of Ballet formed.
	Government of Ireland Act passed.	Lyonel Feininger, *Church*.
		Juan Gris, *Book and Newspaper*.
	Adolf Hitler announces his 25-point programme in Munich.	Maurice Ravel, *La Valse*.

YEAR	AGE	THE LIFE AND THE LAND
1921	50	Costa refuses the Finance portfolio offered to him by Bernardino Machado, and finally returns to Portugal for the first time since 1921, to be present at the burial of Portugal's unknown soldiers.
		Costa is caught up in a financial swindle known as the '$50 million loan'.
		For the first time, the PRP does not win an election, leading to a Liberal government under António Granjo; António de Oliveira Salazar is elected to parliament.
		Costa is also elected to the Chamber of Deputies by Lisbon, but does not take up his seat.
		Oct: Republican 'purists' overthrow the government but lose control of events; Granjo and other leading political figures are murdered; foreign governments threaten to intervene to restore order.
1922	51	Period of relative political calm begins under António Maria da Silva.
		Costa is elected to the Chamber of Deputies by Lisbon, but does not take up his seat and refuses to form a government.

YEAR	HISTORY	CULTURE
1921	Irish Free State established.	Aldous Huxley, *Crome Yellow*.
	Peace treaty signed between Russia and Germany.	D H Lawrence, *Women in Love*.
	State of Emergency proclaimed in Germany in the face of economic crisis.	Prokofiev, *The Love for Three Oranges*.
	Washington Naval Treaty signed.	
1922	Britain recognises Kingdom of Egypt under Fuad I.	T S Eliot, *The Waste Land*.
	Election in Irish Free State gives majority to Pro-Treaty candidates. IRA takes large areas under its control.	James Joyce, *Ulysses*.
		F Scott Fitzgerald, *The Beautiful and Damned*.
	League of Nations council approves British mandate in Palestine.	British Broadcasting Company (later Corporation) (BBC) founded: first radio broadcasts.

YEAR	AGE	THE LIFE AND THE LAND
1923	52	Costa is elected to the Directorate of the PRP, but refuses to participate in its proceedings.
		Manuel Teixeira Gomes is elected President of the Republic.
		With Teixeira Gomes' support, Costa attempts to form a 'National' government, but fails to attract the support of all the major parties and quits.
1924	53	Costa is elected to the Directorate of the PRP, but refuses to participate in party life; a second attempt to form a 'National' government is quickly abandoned.
1925	54	Costa is elected to the Directorate of the PRP, but refuses to participate in party life; refuses as well a party request to form a government.
		Political instability returns.
		Apr: Military coup fails – and leaders go unpunished.
		Costa leads Portugal's delegation to the League of Nations; he leads the negotiating team trying to reach a settlement with Great Britain over Portugal's war debt. He is elected to the Chamber of Deputies, but does not take up his seat.

YEAR	HISTORY	CULTURE
1923	French and Belgian troops occupy the Ruhr when Germany fails to make reparation payments. The USSR formally comes into existence. Wilhelm Marx succeeds Stresemann as German Chancellor. State of Emergency declared in Germany. British Mandate in Palestine begins. Adolf Hitler's *coup d'état* (The Beer Hall Putsch) fails.	P G Wodehouse, *The Inimitable Jeeves.* George Gershwin, *Rhapsody in Blue.* Bela Bartok, *Dance Suite.* BBC listings magazine *Radio Times* first published.
1924	Death of Lenin. Dawes Plan published. Greece is proclaimed a republic. Nazi party enters the Reichstag with 32 seats for the first time, after the elections to the German parliament.	E M Forster, *A Passage to India.* George Bernard Shaw, *St Joan.* 'The Blue Four' expressionist group is formed. George Braque, *Sugar Bowl.* Fernand Leger, *Ballet Mecanique.*
1925	Pound Sterling returns to the Gold Standard. Paul von Hindenburg, former military leader, is elected President of Germany. Locarno Treaty signed in London.	Franz Kafka, *The Trial.* Virginia Woolf, *Mrs Dalloway.* Film: *Battleship Potemkin.*

YEAR	AGE	THE LIFE AND THE LAND
1926	55	Costa is elected President of the League of Nations Assembly during the extraordinary session held to discuss German accession; returns to Portugal for the last time in his life.
		28 May: Military coup brings the First Republic to an end. Long power struggle ensues, leading to the triumph of General Óscar Fragoso Carmona, who becomes President.
1927	56	Major republican revolt is crushed.
		Costa co-founds the League for the Defence of the Republic.
1928	57	Salazar is appointed Finance Minister in a military-led cabinet.
1931	60	Costa is present at the Beyris meeting which re-launches the exiled opposition after a number of failed risings.

YEAR	HISTORY	CULTURE
1926	General Strike in Great Britain.	A A Milne, *Winnie the Pooh*.
	France proclaims the Lebanon as a republic.	Ernest Hemingway, *The Sun Also Rises*.
	Germany is admitted into the League of Nations.	Sean O'Casey, *The Plough and The Stars*.
	In the USSR, Trotsky and Zinoviev are expelled from Politburo of Communist Party, following Stalin's victory.	Oscar Kokoschka, *Terrace in Richmond*.
		Edvard Munch, *The Red House*.
		Eugene D'Albert, *The Golem*.
		Film: *The General*.
1927	Inter-Allied military control of Germany ends.	Marcel Proust, *Le Temps retrouve*.
	Britain recognises rule of Ibn Saud in the Hejaz.	Adolf Hitler, *Mein Kampf*.
		Film: *The Jazz Singer*.
1928	Transjordan becomes self-governing under the British Mandate.	D H Lawrence, *Lady Chatterley's Lover*.
	Kellogg-Briand Pact outlawing war and providing for peaceful settlement of disputes, is signed.	Henri Matisse, *Seated Odalisque*.
		George Gershwin, *An American in Paris*.
		Kurt Weill, *The Threepenny Opera*.
1931	Delhi Pact between the Viceroy of India and Gandhi suspends the civil disobedience campaign.	Robert Frost, *Collected Poems*.
		Gershwin, *Of thee I sing*.
	Bankruptcy of Credit-Anstalt in Austria begins financial collapse of Central Europe.	Salvador Dali, *The Persistence of Memory*.
		Max Beckmann, *Still Life with Studio Window*.

YEAR	AGE	THE LIFE AND THE LAND
1932	61	Salazar is invited by Carmona to form a government, the first civilian cabinet since 1926.
1933	62	The constitution of Salazar's New State is approved by national referendum.
		Costa is interviewed by Brazilian journalist José Jobim, leading to the publication of *A Verdade Sobre Salazar* [The Truth About Salazar].
1936	65	Costa helps to create a Portuguese Popular Front.
		Salazar provides logistical and political aid to Spanish rebels, inaugurating a policy of cooperation with Franco that will last over three decades.

YEAR	HISTORY	CULTURE
1932	Germany withdraws temporarily from the Geneva Disarmament Conference. Britain, France, Germany and Italy make the 'No Force Declaration', renouncing the use of force for settling differences.	Brecht, *St Joan of the Slaughterhouses.* Aldous Huxley, *Brave New World.* Pablo Picasso, *Head of a Woman.* Sergei Prokofiev, *Piano Concerto No. 5 in G major Op. 55.*
1933	Adolf Hitler is appointed Chancellor of Germany. Germany withdraws from League of Nations and Disarmament Conference.	George Orwell, *Down and Out in Paris and London.* Matisse, *The Dance.* All modernist German art suppressed in favour of superficial realism. Richard Strauss, *Arabella.*
1936	German troops occupy Rhineland. Abdication Crisis. Outbreak of Spanish Civil War. Mussolini proclaims the Rome-Berlin Axis. Amy Johnson flies from England to Cape Town.	J M Keynes, *General Theory of Employment, Interest and Money.* Prokofiev, *Peter and the Wolf.* Penguin Books starts paperback revolution. Berlin Olympics. BBC begins world's first television transmission service.

YEAR	AGE	THE LIFE AND THE LAND
1937	66	Costa is named Masonic Grandmaster, but never takes up his position
		11 May: Costa dies at the Hotel Vernet, Paris.
1939–45		Salazar preserves Portuguese neutrality during the Second World War.

YEAR	HISTORY	CULTURE
1937	UK royal commission on Palestine recommends partition into British and Arab areas and Jewish state. Italy joins German-Japanese Anti-Comintern Pact. Irish Free State becomes Eire under de Valera's Irish Constitution.	George Orwell, *The Road to Wigan Pier*. Fernand Leger, *Le Transport des Forces*. Picasso, *Guernica*. Jean-Paul Sartre, *Nausea*. John Steinbeck, *Of Mice and Men*. Nylon patented in USA.
1939–45	Second World War. 1945: Germans surrender on Italian front. Hitler commits suicide in Berlin, and the city surrenders to Soviets. USA drops atomic bombs on Hiroshima and Nagasaki. Japan surrenders to Allies.	1939: James Joyce, *Finnegan's Wake*. 1940: Ernest Hemingway, *For Whom the Bell Tolls*. 1942: Shostakovich, *Symphony No. 7*. 1943: Henry Moore, *Madonna and Child*. 1944: T S Eliot, *Four Quartets*. Terrence Rattigan, *The Winslow Boy*.Tennessee Williams, *The Glass Menagerie*. 1945: George Orwell, *Animal Farm*. Jean-Paul Sartre, *The Age of Reason*. Evelyn Waugh, *Brideshead Revisited*.

YEAR	AGE	THE LIFE AND THE LAND
1970		Salazar is forced to retire due to illness in 1968, and dies two years later.
1971		Afonso Costa's remains are reburied in Seia.

YEAR	HISTORY	CULTURE
1970	Golan Heights see severe fighting between Israel and Syria.	Yamasaki, First tower of World Trade Centre completed, New York.
	King Hussein and Yasser Arafat agree peace after Jordanian army ordered to disband PLO in Jordan.	Dario Fo, *Accidental Death of an Anarchist*.
		The Beatles, *Let it Be*.
		The Beatles split up.
	Cambodia declares itself the Khmer Republic.	Jimi Hendrix dies.
	IBM invents the floppy disk.	Films: *Kes. Love Story. Ryan's Daughter*.
1971	Idi Amin seizes power in Uganda.	Shostakovich, *Symphony No. 15*.
	USA ends trade embargo with China.	Godspell, *Jesus Christ Superstar*.
	Indo-Pakistan war: East Pakistan becomes Bangladesh.	Films. *A Clockwork Orange. Death in Venice*.

Further Reading

Research for this book was based almost entirely on primary sources. The most important of these were the holdings of the Arquivo Histórico Diplomático, housed in Lisbon, at the Ministério dos Negócios Estrangeiros (MNE). It contains the voluminous correspondence between the Portuguese delegation to the Peace Conference and officials at the MNE, the Secretariat of the Peace Conference, and other delegations. It also contains the handwritten minutes of the delegation's meetings, where strategy was discussed and complaints were aired. Some of Afonso Costa's official correspondence from Paris has found its way to the Arquivo Histórico Militar, also in Lisbon. A small part of his private correspondence, mostly with members of his family, can be consulted at the Fundação Mário Soares. This collection includes the brief biography he began when jailed in Elvas, the source of much of our knowledge about his childhood. Costa's 'subversive' activity after 1926 was followed by the New State's secret police, the Polícia de Vigilância e Defesa do Estado, whose archive is housed in the National Archive, in Lisbon. The more important aspects of this activity rose up the chain of command all the way to Salazar himself, and can be consulted in his archive, also located in the National Archive. Of great use in trying to make sense of Portuguese politics are the views of Lisbon-based diplomats. British and French diplomatic reports, to be found in the National Archives, London, and the archives of the Ministère des Affaires Etrangères, Paris, were used in this book.

The earlier parts of Costa's political career can be traced through a number of easily accessed sources. AH de Oliveira Marques performed an invaluable service in this regard, publishing many of them. His *Afonso Costa* (Arcádia, Lisbon: 1972) is a good starting place. Costa's parliamentary interventions are best read as part of on-going debates, and these are now available online in their totality at debates.parlamento.pt. Oliveira Marques also headed the team that edited an invaluable reference work: *Parlamentares e Ministros da Primeira República (1910–1926)* (Assembleia da República/ Afrontamento, Lisbon: 2000).

Afonso Costa often mentioned the desire to write his memoirs in order to make clear once and for all why Portugal had to intervene in the First World War and to participate actively in the fighting on the Western Front. He never wrote this book, however, and seems not to have written a final report on his activities in Paris. There are, however, a number of other memoirs and diaries that shed light on this period of Portuguese history. The most significant, in many ways, is that of General Tamagnini de Abreu, the commander-in-chief of the Portuguese Expeditionary Corps to France. This was recently identified and published by Isabel Pestana Marques as *Memórias do General, 1915–1919* (Fundação Mariana Seixas, Viseu: 2004). Others include António José de Almeida, *Quarenta Anos de Vida Literária e Política*, 4 Vols (J Rodrigues, Lisbon: 1934); Manuel de Arriaga, *Na*

Primeira Presidência da República Portuguesa: Um Rápido Relatório (Livraria Clássica Editora, Lisbon: 1916); João Chagas, *Diário*, 4 Vols (Edições Rolim, Lisbon: 1986); Jaime Cortesão, *Memórias da Grande Guerra* (Renascença Portuguesa, Oporto: 1919); José Mendes Ribeiro Norton de Matos, *Memórias e Trabalhos da Minha Vida*, 4 Vols, (Editora Marítimo-Colonial, Lisbon: 1944); and Egas Moniz, *Um Ano de Política* (Portugal-Brasil, Lisbon: 1919).

The press played a vital role in the life of the First Republic. All parties and factions, no matter how small, had their own newspapers, and freedom of the press was absolute. For this book I have relied on two Lisbon-based news dailies, *Diário de Notícias* and *O Século*, and the republican press's flagship, *O Mundo*, for which Afonso Costa wrote under the pseudonym 'Stry'. *The Times* and *Le Temps* are indispensable tools in following the Peace Conference and assessing Afonso Costa's claims of international recognition for his work.

The period immediately preceding the Republic is made sense of by Rui Ramos in his *D. Carlos* (Temas e Debates, Lisbon: 2007). 2010 will see Portugal marking the Republic's centenary, and historiographical attention will be focused on the First Republic as never before. A number of new assessments of the regime are in production. The first of these, published as this volume was being concluded, is Fernando Rosas and Maria Fernanda Rollo (eds), *História da Primeira República Portuguesa* (Tinta da China, Lisbon: 2009). Many more will follow in the two or three years to come. This is good news, because there is still much to learn about the First Republic, its leaders and its parties.

There are relatively few contemporary sources in English that cover the First Republic in any great detail, and with sufficient understanding of the motives behind republican policy. Of these, the most satisfactory is George Young's *Portugal Old and Young: An Historical Study* (Clarendon Press, Oxford: 1917). Young, a British diplomat stationed in Lisbon, was unusually open-minded and even sympathetic towards a political project which most of his contemporaries viewed with distrust. English-language secondary sources are more numerous, but generally dispersed. For an account of Portugal's involvement in the First World War see my own *Portugal 1914–1926: From the First World War to Military Dictatorship* (Bristol: Hiplam, 2004). An article published by Manuel Baiôa, Paulo Jorge Fernandes and myself, 'The political history of twentieth-century Portugal', *E-Journal of Portuguese History*, 1 (2003), is a useful introduction to Portuguese politics in the 20th century. Others include Tom Gallagher's *Portugal: A Twentieth Century Interpretation* (Manchester University Press, Manchester: 1983) and R A H Robinson's *Contemporary Portugal: A History* (Allen & Unwin, London: 1979). Douglas L Wheeler was one of the pioneers of contemporary Portuguese studies. His *Republican Portugal: A Political History, 1910–1926* (University of Wisconsin Press, Madison: 1978) remains an important port of call for a student of the regime. Of Portuguese historians based in Portugal, none more than António Costa Pinto is concerned with making Portuguese history available in English. His edited volume *Contemporary Portugal: Politics, Society and Culture* (Social Science Monographs, Boulder: 2003) is a good place to start any investigation.

Picture Sources

The author and publishers wish to express their thanks to the following sources of illustrative material and/or permission to reproduce it. They will make proper acknowledgements in future editions in the event that any omissions have occurred.

Courtesy of Topham Picturepoint.

Endpapers
The Signing of Peace in the Hall of Mirrors, Versailles, 28th June 1919 by Sir William Orpen (Imperial War Museum: Bridgeman Art Library)
Front row: Dr Johannes Bell (Germany) signing with Herr Hermann Müller leaning over him
Middle row (seated, left to right): General Tasker H Bliss, Col E M House, Mr Henry White, Mr Robert Lansing, President Woodrow Wilson (United States); M Georges Clemenceau (France); Mr David Lloyd George, Mr Andrew Bonar Law, Mr Arthur J Balfour, Viscount Milner, Mr G N Barnes (Great Britain); Prince Saionji (Japan)
Back row (left to right): M Eleftherios Venizelos (Greece);

Dr Afonso Costa (Portugal); Lord Riddell (British Press); Sir George E Foster (Canada); M Nikola Pašić (Serbia); M Stephen Pichon (France); Col Sir Maurice Hankey, Mr Edwin S Montagu (Great Britain); the Maharajah of Bikaner (India); Signor Vittorio Emanuele Orlando (Italy); M Paul Hymans (Belgium); General Louis Botha (South Africa); Mr W M Hughes (Australia)

Jacket images

(Front): Imperial War Museum: akg Images.
(Back): *Peace Conference at the Quai d'Orsay* by Sir William Orpen (Imperial War Museum: akg Images).
Left to right (seated): Signor Orlando (Italy); Mr Robert Lansing, President Woodrow Wilson (United States); M Georges Clemenceau (France); Mr David Lloyd George, Mr Andrew Bonar Law, Mr Arthur J Balfour (Great Britain); Left to right (standing): M Paul Hymans (Belgium); Mr Eleftherios Venizelos (Greece); The Emir Feisal (The Hashemite Kingdom); Mr W F Massey (New Zealand); General Jan Smuts (South Africa); Col E M House (United States); General Louis Botha (South Africa); Prince Saionji (Japan); Mr W M Hughes (Australia); Sir Robert Borden (Canada); Mr G N Barnes (Great Britain); M Ignacy Paderewski (Poland)

Index